RESTITUTION
AND HOW TO OBTAIN IT

HOW TO LITIGATE
SUCCESSFULLY

PHILIP SINEL

R^ethink

First published in Great Britain in 2021
by Rethink Press (www.rethinkpress.com)

Contents

Introduction

The genesis for this book came from three recent cases that I dealt with on behalf of clients: two of my clients were situated in Jersey, which is where our chambers have been based for a number of years, the third was resident in Kenya. I almost called the book $1\frac{1}{2} = 45$ for reasons that will become clear later on.

The background that all three clients shared was that they had been defrauded by a clearing bank, or by a subsidiary of one, or by both. These were substantial claims for otherwise profitable businesses that were all family-owned (dependent on one or two family members for direction). They had all been significantly disadvantaged; one was facing the spectre of both corporate and personal insolvency, the others had lost large sums of cash, and/or were prevented from refinancing and developing their businesses.

How to turn one-and-a-half million pounds sterling (£1,500,000) into forty-five million pounds sterling (£45,000,000)? One-and-a-half million pounds was spent by the three clients between them on law, intelligence and expert witnesses. Forty-five million pounds sterling (£45,000,000) was the total of the benefits they received. Two of the figures are verifiable, being £15 million and £10 million cash settlements, and the third reliably and conservatively estimated. I attributed this amount as the benefit to the client of cancelling, free of all charges (including redemption charges), the financial instrument holding the client hotelier into a 28-year period, paying 9% on its borrowings, the continuation of which would have sterilised any future development for the business.

This book sets out to show how it is possible to obtain restitution – the repayment of financial damages or losses – should you find itself in similar circumstances to my clients. I should say that this is not a book simply about money although, as the cases above show, the sums involved are often considerable and can have consequences for the survival, or otherwise, of a business.

This book also recognises the human impact of the stresses and strains placed upon legitimate business-people by defaulting business partners or those who simply set out to defraud them. Life for legitimate businesspeople is hard enough. We all have to wade through the issues that life throws at us in relation to our personal lives, as well as in relation to our business lives. We do not need the additional stress of trying to recover money which has been dishonestly extracted from us but, unfortunately, many of us will find ourselves facing one or more of the challenges I mention in this book.

All businesses face challenges, to use a relatively neutral word, in producing a quality saleable product. They have to deal with staff and business partners as well as red tape. After all these challenges, many legitimate businesspeople are ruined and/or lose their livelihoods, their assets and indeed their homes as a result of defaults by third parties which they did not cause or deserve.

Our three sample clients came out well. Their loan-to-value ratios came back to healthy, manageable proportions, their borrowings dropped, their interest rates fell back to comfortable levels and they could, once again, enjoy the fruits of their labour. My firm also worried about the strain on our clients as human beings; thankfully, they are now all doing well.

This is a book about how we did it for them and many others, how you can do it and how anybody in a legal dispute, almost anywhere, can apply the same principles.

It is designed to diffuse the opacity of the process and to help anybody with a valid claim to obtain restitution. If you have ever been to court and lost; or wished you had gone to court but been scared off by the costs, time and money involved; or not known when, how and who to litigate, then this book is for you. I also believe that understanding the restitution process can equip any business owner with foresight to anticipate common pitfalls and arm them with knowledge of what to do should they find themselves in difficulties.

This book is designed to appeal to almost anybody in the Commonwealth or an Anglo-Saxon jurisdiction. It touches on the processes in the USA, to the inadequate extent to which I know about these, and adds helpful pointers in relation to any dispute, anywhere.

I write about matters that I have actually dealt with, which is why you will find real examples throughout the book of problems my firm has solved and the challenges which we and our clients have faced. The idea of producing examples is to underline that this book is not an academic exercise but very much built from a practitioner and/or victim's point of view.

For obvious reasons nothing in this book should be taken as being legal advice *per se*. All disputes turn on their own facts and the law chosen to apply to them, a topic which we deal with later on.

I run a small firm of lawyers based in Jersey, with over thirty years' worth of experience in bringing and defending claims. Jersey, for the uninitiated, is a small island off the coast of England with a quasi-anglicised judicial system and an offshore financial centre which has thrown up a lot of international disputes.

In addition to running litigation in Jersey, the firm runs litigation in other countries as well. We also buy and enforce debt around the world through Sinels Global Restitution Limited, and have a consultancy dealing with both pure and applied intelligence, Sintel Global Limited.

Rule Number One

A constant theme in this book is what I would term Rule Number One – *work backwards from the end*. This rule is so crucial that Rule Number One is not only the first rule, but the paramount rule to stick to in all the matters covered in this book. It is a theme I will come back to many times.

Litigation, like warfare, is costly and truly dreadful at many levels. Despite this, many litigants plunge into the process without knowing where they are going and without any clearly defined aim(s). This is why Rule Number One is so very important.

By working backwards from a clearly defined aim, Rule Number One also requires you to set out at the beginning of the process what constitutes success. What is going to constitute success for you? How is it defined? Is it achievable, and if so, at what cost?

1
Front-End Load

In the Introduction I stressed the importance of what I called Rule Number One: start at the end and work backwards. In this chapter, we look at how that is achieved in practice and some steps along the way. At the end of the chapter, we will take a look at how this plays out in practice.

Before embarking on any complex litigation, the aim of the action needs to be firmly defined, then it can be *front-end loaded*; this step is all too often omitted and even if we acknowledge that 'no battle plan survives the first encounter with the enemy',[1] it needs to be done.

---

1   This is attributed to Rommel but seems to have been said first by a Prussian field marshal, Helmuth von Moltke the Elder, see www .oxfordreference.com/view/10.1093/acref/9780191826719.001.0001 /q-oro-ed4-00007547.

Moreover, setting out with no plan and no front-end load is a bit like wandering across three lanes of traffic with your eyes shut.

There are two types of front-end load, legal and factual. This chapter deals with both. What do we mean by front-end load? An alternative but less satisfactory description might be pre-project planning, or an extension of the well-known 80/20 rule, but in this context, it means two things:

1. Taking steps to make sure the whole enterprise is worth doing, and

2. Giving yourself the best possible chance of achieving victory.

Anecdotal evidence on both sides of the Atlantic suggests that many court judgments and orders are never enforced. Colleagues in the United States of America suggested to me that this might be true of as many as 80% of run-of-the-mill judgment creditors,[2] a position exacerbated by the fact that the USA is a federation of states, each with its own jurisdiction and legal

---

2   A judgment creditor has been awarded money by a court, to be paid by a judgment debtor.

machinery. The states may not (all) be separated by water, but the difficulties remain.

There is a market for uncollected debt: firms buy it and try to collect. My firm Restitution offers this service. When I discuss this with UK colleagues, they are often amazed at how many judgment debts people try to sell to them at face value or close to it. A judgment debt is worthless unless and until you collect it. If the creditor has been unable to collect any money at all, then the first factor to take into the equation is: Has the debtor got any assets that can be 'attached' (or even seized)?[3]

Now remember Rule Number One. Before you go to law, has the other side got any assets and will they still be there at the end of the litigation?

In some cases, for example when you are suing an institution or large company, the answer appears self-evident. Remember, however, by way of risk management, that back in the credit crunch of 2008/9 the Royal Bank of Scotland plc, Lloyds Bank plc, HBOS and Northern Rock were all close to, or actually, insolvent.

---

3   A court may 'attach' an order to an asset, preventing it from being used (or, sometimes, requiring it to be sold) to pay a debt. A court may even seize an asset and sell it.

Food for thought, especially if you buy the 'too big to fail' argument.

A simple rule of thumb, even with large corporate defendants, is to begin by gathering some basic information. A lot is freely available. It may prove to be inaccurate, but it is a start. Also, identify the owners and controllers (which may be surprisingly difficult). As the relative size of the debt increases, and the size of the debtor reduces, the need for information of this nature at the beginning becomes more acute. Litigation is expensive and it takes time. There is no point to the exercise unless it is going to deliver value for money at the end of the day.

This is not a chapter on how to run an intelligence operation, but it is important to briefly look at what information needs to be gathered, step-by-step.

Firstly, as we have already stated, it's crucial to ask 'at the end of the trial will the debtor have enough assets to pay the debt?' If not, are there other assets that could be 'attached', or pressures that can be applied to some other party, to ensure payment? What assets? Other businesses, real estate, machinery? If the answers to all these questions look negative or doubtful at the beginning, then you must consider locking down the potential debtor's assets before you start; or not start at all.

If the company could (or will) be stripped of assets, can 'they' be 'joined' into the action?[4] Will 'they' cut and run? Are there any personal guarantees? If judgment went against 'them', would this prevent 'them' trading in the future? By 'them', I mean the ones who really control things and who end up with the money.

Will it be possible to enforce the judgment in another country where assets exist, if necessary? More importantly, will there be assets? Will the judgment be exportable to a country where assets exist and where pressure can be brought to bear? Sometimes it is necessary to start in a jurisdiction where there are no assets.

All clients, and indeed their advisers, can take some basic steps:

1. Carry out basic Google searches on the target and its directors.

2. Investigate corporate filings; open source material in the UK Companies House can be a mine of helpful information.

---

4   Added to the list of defendants as the action proceeds.

3. Where the target is a qualified person, look for professional filings: for example, has the accountant in question been struck off, in which case what is (s)he doing, where is (s)he living and what is (s)he living off?

4. Carry out literature searches: do not restrict yourself simply to what is on the internet, look at magazines and trade journals in the relevant industry(ies).

5. Speak to other people in the industry who know the firm or person.

6. Former partners, spouses, friends and co-workers can be an invaluable source of information.

7. Consider using private detectives or an intelligence agency: Sinels has an in-house intelligence consultancy, and there are many firms that can help you gather intelligence.

8. Talk both generally and about specifics to the potential target and witnesses and record your conversations; audio recordings are admissible in many countries' courts.

Point 8 is important. Before legal action, both witnesses and defendants can be frank about their actions and what I would term reality: 'Yes, we owe the money' or 'Sorry; we borrowed your money to pay someone else; we will pay you back next week'. Post-litigation excuses tend to be very different to pre-litigation excuses. An admission of indebtedness, or of facts, can be incalculable in value. Unassailable evidence of culpability takes years off the litigation process.

Crooks have strange mindsets: one made an appointment to see me, then confessed fulsomely. His purpose was to deflect liability and blame, but it broke the case wide open. He went on to mount all sorts of denials and legal challenges but he could not put the genie back in the bottle. Sometimes crooks simply do not understand that what they are doing is wrong.

Set out below is an edited transcript of a conversation a creditor had with a debtor. It contains a frank and cheerful admission that money is owing and a promise to pay:

FIRST CONVERSATION

Debtor: Unfortunately, ▇▇▇▇▇▇ has left a large hole – £15 million to be shared between a number of people. The reality of the matter is I am not going to have surplus until the end of the month, which will come from the sale of ▇▇▇▇▇▇.

Creditor: I need a letter from you that I am going to be paid. We are a small firm and two months of work not paid for is something that we cannot sustain.

D: I received a succinct text from you saying you were on holiday so I did not want to bother you until I have sorted this out.

C: I do not want to fall out with you but we need to get paid.

D: I do not want you to fall out with me and I do not want you to bankrupt me either. It is not a large amount of money but the well is dry at the moment…

C: That is money. Can we count on being paid then?

D: I will pay you directly through my solicitor.

SECOND CONVERSATION

Creditor: Hiya ▮▮▮▮▮, where are you?

Debtor: Oh ▮▮▮▮▮, how are you?

C: Sorely oppressed. Which country are you in?

D: I am in Hong Kong at the moment. Yes, it's been a busy old week: been between Dubai, Beijing and Hong Kong, back to Beijing tomorrow and hopefully back to London on Wednesday.

C: Okay.

D: Look, everything should be sorted out next week. If your boys are happier issuing a stat demand well, you know, up to them, both ████ and ████ are due to complete on Friday, but the ████ transaction, which has been the one that dominated this year, the first of these monies moved today.

C: Good.

D: So that will all get completed, I would hope, sort of Wednesday, Thursday or Friday of next week.

C: Okay then; that's cool, I'll hold the dogs off.

D: Yes, yes.

C: Who is going to pay us?

D: Well, it will either come out of my solicitors, as I wrote to you in my email, or it will come straight out of my overseas account because that is where the ████ fee is going.

C: Do you want to give me the details of the solicitor?

D: By all means.

C: Okay, cheers ████.

D: Okay, ████, have a great weekend.

C: When are you back?

D: Crack of dawn on Wednesday is the plan.

C: I am over Friday but fairly chocker.

D: You never know, you might want to come and collect the cheque.

C: Cheers, ▇▇▇▇▇.

In the litigation, the debtor maintained that the debt was not due and that payment had not been promised. With hindsight, we decided that the admission and promises had been intended to put payment off. The admission enabled the creditor to speed up collection and all funds owed were received in weeks.

Legal front-end load

At the outset of any properly or ideally run action, armed with as complete a set of facts as can be mustered, you need to take legal advice as to what you have to prove in law in order to win.

Pleadings are dealt with in Chapter 3 but many legal textbooks set out the basics, ie what needs to be proved to sustain the claim. This book is a layman's guide, not a technical exposition, but we thought it would be helpful to give a checklist of what they cover, to show that the process should not be shrouded in mystery.

Contract

This is fairly straightforward: was there an agreement and what were its terms? Has it been breached? Has this resulted in loss?

Conspiracy

This word is often misunderstood. Set out below is what you actually have to plead, and therefore prove. If you do not have all the evidence to prove every part, you are going to have to think very carefully about making an allegation, let alone litigating it. Conspiracy is overused and little understood by non-lawyers, but also one of the least understood and most underused weapons in the litigation armoury. I include it here to show what legal front-end loading is and how it can work in practice.

Different types of conspiracy. Conspiracy is 'the agreement of two or more to do an unlawful act, or to do a lawful act by unlawful means'.[5] Historically, there are two kinds of conspiracy, the elements of which are distinct:

1. 'Unlawful means': the participants combine to perform acts which are themselves unlawful, using unlawful means.

2. A combination to perform acts which, although not themselves unlawful, are done with the sole or main purpose of injuring a third party: 'it is in the fact of the conspiracy that the unlawfulness resides'.[6]

Necessary elements of an action in conspiracy. You must prove four 'necessary elements':

1. combination or agreement (see next section) between two or more individuals (required for both types of conspiracy);

2. An intent to injure (required for both types of conspiracy but must be shown as the sole or main purpose for type (2) above – 'injure' here refers to financial harm);

---

5   *Mulcahy v R* (1868) LR 3 HL 306.
6   Lord Watson in *Allen v Flood* [1898] at 108.

3. Under this combination or agreement and with that intention the acts were carried out (prove what they were and whether they took place); and

4. Resulting in loss and damage to the claimant (you).

Combination or agreement. This could be an express agreement, or something much less formal. The court looks at the overt acts and infers from them that there was agreement to further the shared object of the combination.

The point of this slightly complex example is to show that in most jurisdictions you can work out in advance what you need to allege and the evidence that you will need to succeed at trial. An ill-thought-out allegation or a vaguely defined claim can go badly wrong.

Let us take another example, a simple one going back to breach of contract. You think a contract has been breached or, more likely, 'This happened; have I got a remedy?' It is easy if there is a written contract, but many contracts are made orally, or follow exchanges of letters/emails, so you then need to show that you have performed your part; each part needs to be set out in some detail. A contract is an agreement to do something for reward. If it was not written down, many people fail to take legal action when an agreement is broken, when in fact ample evidence might exist, both of its terms and that it was performed.

In court, your lawyer's closing speech, in essence, will be based on the pleadings, which set out the constituent parts of the allegations that need to be proven. This is then cross-referred to the evidence. I suggest that, in effect, you write your closing speech at the start of the case. Often this will not be perfect, but it is a good and necessary discipline.

Back to basics and front-end load. When you first see your lawyer (or shortly thereafter) you should be as organised as possible. A team who can pre-assemble facts and documents is well in front.

You can pay lawyers high hourly rates to do this or get a large part of it right yourself. Most people can do most or all of preparing:

1. A narrative of what happened, when and who did what, with as many dates as possible;

2. A statement of what you are claiming and why you want to bring a claim, ie why do you claim to be entitled to claim?

3. A basic time-line and dates;

4. An organised set of relevant papers, all the important ones stripped of repetition and duplication;

5. A list of documents (the ones you know about), both those you hold and those held by the opposition (see the section on discovery in Chapter 3); and

6. A list of witnesses: What do they know? Whose side are they on? Which witnesses can the opposition rely on?

Any major piece of litigation should happen in several stages. First you should decide whether it is worth spending money on having an independent expert assess the claim. Does it pass a basic 'smell test'? Might it be sustainable? If it falls down at that stage do not waste any further time with it. Do not expose yourself to an expensive court case you cannot win.

The initial 'due diligence' on a claim is cheap and tends to be in the thousands, not in the tens of thousands,[7] compared to total potential litigation costs, even on

---

7   'Due diligence' means making sure sufficient evidence exists, that it will support your case (ie does it back up what you say?) and may include an assessment of the opposition case.

a big claim. The idea is to work out before starting whether the litigation is feasible or potentially feasible or not.

Factual front-end load

Once the initial appraisal has been made then the front-end load starts. Ideally, it should be started before the other side is aware that steps are being taken. Now is the time to gather and assess evidence. On a big claim, this can be quite expensive but it needs to be done (if possible) before making contact with the opposition.

At this stage it is important to have a fairly clear idea of the value of the claim. The front-end load should not be disproportionate and it comes at a cost that may not be recoverable if the defendant pays what they owe prior to litigation. A lot depends on the type of action: some actions have 'will not pay/settle' written all over them at the start, others admit a more nuanced approach.

You naturally want claims settled as soon as possible, and in many Anglo-Saxon countries strict pre-action protocols try to achieve this. In any event, to engage pre-action meaningfully, you need a good understanding of the case and the legal basis for the claim. This also gives the chance of recovery without full-blown litigation being necessary.

Front-end loading a case is not inconsistent with pre-action protocols or trying to keep costs down. On the contrary, not preparing a case thoroughly may see an action start that should not, which risks wasting costs and possibly the court awarding adverse cost orders against you. If the initial decision-making process is as informed as possible, less is left to chance in a process which, by any stretch of the imagination, involves many uncertainties.

I deal in Chapter 6 with financing your litigation but important points on costs should be mentioned now. As their costs can be disproportionate, thought needs to be put into both the discovery (showing the other side what you have) and the inspection (examining what the other side produces) (see Chapter 3). The knowledge and qualifications of the persons involved need to be thought about: there is no point in using a fee earner at £500/hr to list documents, but considerable point to having highly qualified people decide what is/is not disclosable and review the other side's documentation to see both what is relevant and what has been missed.

Cases can be both won and lost at this stage and judges can become unhappy if they think a party has withheld documentation.

More importantly, thought needs to be deployed before the opposition's list is received. What documentation should they be disclosing? This is perhaps best illustrated by real-life examples.

EXPERT KNOWLEDGE

Our firm, on behalf of a client, accused a financial corporation of:

1. Artificially inflating the price of certain products that its parent had sold to a subsidiary, which was the trustee of the client's family trust;

2. Making so much on these transactions that they were, in effect, paying a kickback to the trustee; and

3. Paying staggering bonuses to employees for selling junk to in-house managers.

At an early stage we worked out exactly where and on what part of the system the defendant had stored the incriminating evidence. We then told the defendant we knew. The case settled on happy terms not long after.

UNPREPAREDNESS

My firm sued a large organisation that had failed to complete a property acquisition. The contract contained a penalty clause, so non-completion without cause meant damages. The institution called as witnesses lawyers, accountants and advisers, none of whom seemed to know exactly why the company had taken the decision it did (various efforts were made to find excuses and blame our client). These witnesses waffled for hours.

The organisation's last witness was its general manager, who knew all about running the business but nothing about the litigation: he had not been prepared and his own lawyers clearly had not spoken to him beforehand, ie, they did not know what he would say. When I asked him why his company had not completed, he said – truthfully – that 'it no longer suited our purpose' – a seminal moment in the case.

CONCLUSION

Preparedness dictates success or the absence of it.

2

Post-Judgment Enforcement

Why is post-judgment enforcement Chapter 2? Because unless you can be sure of enforcing, there is no point in starting the journey. A judgment is a piece of paper; unless it can be turned into money or something else of value, it has no value and it can cost a lot of money to obtain.

Unless your opponent is an obvious payer, eg an institution or similar with sufficient resources, this is something to investigate at the start and keep an eye on during the process. Moreover, some defendants will view a judgment as a starting point for a downward negotiation.

As set out in the Introduction, always start at the end and work backwards. Although we are now looking at the position after judgment, the enforcement equation needs to be examined at the start. Do not waste time and money running a claim unless it will result in a net benefit.

How much?

Most judgments come with the interest attached, ie a figure for the interest on the debt up to the date of judgment. This is important: English courts give a standard 8%. Even on relatively modest debts, it starts to make a difference; if your debtor defaults, or hides, or simply cannot be found, or in any litigation (which takes time), it makes a big difference. Five years at 8% simple interest is 40% of the principal. The first point therefore is to make sure that you claim interest. The second point is to make sure you have an interest-bearing judgment, ie that interest runs until payment, not just up to the date of the judgment.

Some contracts have built-in interest clauses that include default provisions, eg 15% until date of payment. Courts can be inconsistent in their treatment of such clauses. If you put a higher rate of interest in the contract than you would ordinarily be granted in a judgment, ask for contract-rate interest until the date of judgment. The judge might not agree, but if you do not ask for it, you certainly will not get it.

In Anglo-Saxon/Commonwealth countries, judgments come with costs orders attached (more on this in the next section). Systems elsewhere sometimes award costs orders; so how much is your judgment worth and when will you learn what the figure is? Add costs to interest, and ask for interest to be added to costs.

Sometimes courts adjudicate first upon liability and then on the amount. If you have a judgment on liability, this is a good time to reassess the enforcement equation and, if the circumstances merit it, to start locking down the debtor's assets. You know you are entitled to get something, now you need to make sure you actually get paid. All situations are fact-dependent but an early step can be simply to ask for undertakings that assets will not be shuffled (ie dissipated or rearranged) so as to put them beyond creditor reach. This may or may not focus the opposition's mind on what next, on how to avoid insolvency and, hopefully, on payment.

An unpaid judgment can be converted into seizure of goods and money and/or insolvency within a matter of weeks, sometimes days.

If the opposition is an individual, at this stage think about (a) what they have, and (b) what they used to have. The 'what did they have and where did it go' equation can be very important. Even where you ask for an undertaking and get a raspberry, it is not wasted effort as there is now a paper trail; anything done after this request has been flagged will be viewed in a different and more inquisitive light by the courts.

Most legal systems allow for claw-backs/reversals of gratuitous transactions (ie transactions where no or little value is received in return). One obvious example is when a husband transfers all his assets to his wife shortly after he is notified of your claim. Both before and after judgment, putting third-party holders on notice may concentrate the opposition's mind wonderfully. If the potential or actual debtor and the third party both know that asset shuffling is not going to yield any benefits, this may lead to swift resolution.

The position in relation to corporate debtors can be more complicated but the same first steps apply: What has it got? What did it have? Can you get a charge over property or plant as a *quid pro quo* for not provoking a bankruptcy? What does the balance sheet look like? Has the company been milked or otherwise misman-aged by the directors? Did they artificially manipulate the balance sheet, take the money out, then decide to let the company go?

In the latter case, threatening claims against the directors, or even their spouses, may inject much needed reality into the situation. If the company has nothing but Mrs Director has a new Range Rover, there are some obvious questions to ask.

Clearly, you should not begin looking at these questions only after judgment. Post-judgment litigation can be an expensive way to stake a reprieve. 'Reprieve staking' is a gambling term for putting more money in after the initial gamble or series of gambles has failed to pay off. 'One more gamble' might pay off, but the odds have probably not changed.

Costs

English and anglicised courts are becoming increasingly robust about summarily assessing costs (ie giving you a costs figure on the spot or at least shortly after judgment) but you can still have, in effect, two judgments: the first for a sum of money and the second for an unliquidated sum represented by the untaxed orders. The system, in many countries, remains one of taxation, pursuant to which a court-mandated costs assessment is carried out by, hopefully, a qualified clerk who goes through the winning parties claim for costs and in effect makes reductions based on what (s)he thinks should have been charged. That process remains riddled with complexity, arbitrary criteria and delay. In some countries this process can take over a year to complete.

When presented with a bill of costs the opposition, if sensible, make an offer to pay early, to avoid prolonging the case (and further expense). Some dig their heels in and waste as much time and money as they can. The more robust the judiciary, the less progress will be made.

Judgments that need to be enforced across a border bring additional problems. Lawyers in 'civil law' jurisdictions, in particular, do not understand the system of taxation and then query whether the first judgment is final and therefore capable of enforcement. What needs to be explained is that you have got two final judgments, both of which are final and neither of which is susceptible, at that stage, to appeal.

Generally civil law countries adopt a robust system once you get judgment(s) – and sometimes before – and this can be simpler than Anglo-Saxon systems. Some countries enable you to go direct to what they term *Exequatur*; the machinery can take time but once successfully invoked, their system tends to brook little argument.

How hard to push?

Enforcement is voluntary or involuntary. Voluntary enforcement, which is sometimes much better than involuntary enforcement, involves some communication with the debtor. If in negotiation the debtor (perhaps via a third party) suggests they would like to (or admit that they need to) pay, but cannot immediately, you need to find out what they have, ie they need to put their cards on the table in some fashion.

In my experience no debtor is keen on this; transparency is resisted. Some jurisdictions allow for the debtor to be 'examined' after judgment in relation to their assets, which means that you can obtain bank statements, credit card statements and related, as well as asking pointed questions.

Determined debtors and fraudsters have in common a sense of unreality – part of the psyche is missing. They do not see the train coming down the tracks until it has almost arrived. If you are negotiating, or hoping to, this is a form of brinkmanship: the usual rule is that perseverance pays.

If you cannot reach accord, the next step (in many cases best not to hesitate) is involuntary enforcement. This means seizing some assets and selling them for cash. If that is not successful, the next step is bankruptcy proceedings which, almost everywhere, means that all the debtor's assets are transferred to a third party (eg a receiver, liquidator or trustee) who is charged with turning them into cash; but this can be subject to delays, complications and expenses. Particularly in corporate bankruptcies, side agreements can affect who is entitled to draw their charges from these assets, and what priority will be given to different types of debt. Some creditors may have older and larger debts, security may have been offered over some (meaning that assets have already been assigned against the debt), some may enjoy a priority conferred by law (for example, taxes and other amounts owed to the government). It goes without saying that, if there is a bankruptcy, the goose that might have laid the golden egg is now definitely dead, so bankruptcy is a last resort. Bankruptcy is worth a chapter on its own, perhaps for a future edition.

The object of negotiation and appraisal is to obtain more than you would by other means and while, in some cases, there may be human reasons for not extracting all that you are entitled to, in other cases the debtor deserves what is coming to them.

In the meantime, if you have seized an asset what is it worth? Ordinarily it is worth what it will fetch at an auction run by a court-mandated enforcement agency, where every bidder is looking for a bargain. Depending on the nature of the asset, it may be worth talking to the receiver/sheriff/viscount about how the sale is to be carried out. There is no point putting the shares in a specialised, small-cap, private company up for auction in the *Devon & Torquay Gazette*; this is clearly a specialised asset with a limited number of parties who might be interested and they certainly will not be reading the local paper.

In practice I have found receivers/sheriffs/viscounts almost always happy to delegate the sale of specialist items to specialist providers, so long as they have a paper trail which shows that they took logical steps to achieve the best value.

Some examples in practice

First, here are two small, practical examples.

SELLING A BOAT

We seized a boat in poor condition. Before sale, the sheriff allowed us to tidy it up, ie, start the engines to prove they worked, charge the batteries to prove that the electrics worked and power-wash it to make it look better.

We were then allowed to set a reserve price at the auction, based on obvious comparables for that make and year. The boat failed to sell at auction. We subsequently achieved double the price offered at auction by private negotiation with the top bidder.

A SMALL COMPANY'S SHARES

An insouciant small trader owned a private company with 5,000 shares issued with a face value of £1.00 each. He said 'So what?' when we seized the shares. He was very cocky. He said, 'Nobody is going to pay even £1.00 for the shares in that company, even at auction; it only has value to me.' However, we knew that he needed the company because it had third-party contracts. The creditor's response was to say, 'I am sending a friend of mine to the auction, who will bid the amount of the debt.' At that stage the penny dropped and the debtor paid in cash.

Let us say you have obtained judgment against an obviously affluent defendant, or have reached agreement with someone who can afford it all at once or in stages. Normally, if agreement is reached, then you know when and how you are going to get paid. Remember, you have not been paid until the money arrives and there can be all sorts of unexpected interventions. Security is good if you are taking stage payments. It is a prudent step but, unless you know exactly what assets and income the opposition have, proceed with caution lest they change their mind or have other huge debts which trigger insolvency.

Proceeding with caution means acting like a prudent lender. If what you are owed is not all coming at once then you are in a similar position to a lender. Look for security and build in penalties for default so, if instalments do not arrive, the rate of interest increases and/or the whole amount becomes due immediately.

A DIFFICULT MAN

My firm recently dealt with a multimillionaire who refused to pay a judgment obtained in Country A.

The amount was around £250,000, small change to him. He had a history of not paying a whole range of suppliers: building a picture was not hard. Fortunately, for various reasons, we had acquired a good road map of his business and personal assets.

Moving jurisdiction was an issue. Before we launched the action in Country B (in which he lived and we knew he had some assets), we also researched his recent activity in Country C. This meant that we knew where shares, investment portfolios and cash were held, where some valuable cars were registered (Country B) and where they were garaged (Country C).

Given how much he owed and how much we knew, it took a surprising amount of push and shove to get paid. Knowing that there were assets including bank accounts in Country B, we first had to apply from the court that issued the judgment to a higher court, so that automatic reciprocation provisions between Countries B and C would cover it, which would potentially save a lot of time and costs.

We invoked the reciprocal powers in Country B, which involved serving notice during which time he left Country B and cleared out most of his bank accounts. Most of his other assets in Country B had been awarded to his wife. We then moved to Country C, obtained another judgment (reciprocally) and obtained ancillary court orders, specifically targeting his company's investment portfolio and taking possession of the cars, simultaneously obtaining their ownership documents through the Vehicle Registry in Country B.

At this very late stage, he finally contacted my client and made assurances of payment. Not unnaturally, their trust in his *bona fides* had expired, along with their patience. We kept the portfolio blocked and also custody of the vehicles, then asked for and received sums in escrow to cover court fees and legal costs for the assessment or 'taxation' period.[8]

Having wasted tens of thousands by avoiding payment and racking up interest, court and legal costs in three jurisdictions, he employed lawyers and a costs draftsman to argue about each line of these bills. That operation cost him more than he saved. Some debtors are irrational to the last.

LONG HAUL

We bought a debt from a finance house. The debtor had borrowed money to buy a fancy car for her toy-boy in Country A. Her application for credit listed a number of offshore accounts in the names of shell companies.

---

8 An 'escrow' arrangement means a third party is given money or property that can only be used for certain very tightly defined purposes.

Step one was to recapture the vehicle and sell it. There was a shortfall so we set about recovering the balance. The debtor claimed to live in Country B.

After a lot of digging, we found she was not resident in Country B, did not live or trade there, but was in fact a successful property developer living in Country C who had put all her deals into offshore structures along with her house.

This loan had been issued in Country D so we had to start there: the contract had an exclusive jurisdiction clause. We served via her lawyers in Country B, obtained judgment in Country D and, after some resistance, then launched another action in Country C where, on the face of it, she owned nothing in her own name.

Our intelligence proved good; matters resolved themselves when a young bailiff rang to tell us he was standing next to the lady's sports car, and asked what he should do next.

'If the keys are in it, drive it away,' I replied. 'If not, put it on a flat-back.'

At this stage the property developer finally decided enough was enough and paid in cash, on the spot. I have since wondered how she came to be holding that much cash.

CONCLUSION

Remember Rule Number One: start at the end and work backwards.

3
The Litigation Process – What Happens

In the beginning

Nearly all claims, except where there is a need for urgent *ex parte* relief,[9] start with a letter of demand sent to ask for 'relief' from something, eg payment due under a contract but not made. Letters exchanged at this stage can be as helpful or as unhelpful and silly and wasteful as the opposition wants to make them. Sometimes an application comes back with threats, leading the author to think cynically about how much the lawyers on the other side are budgeting on earning out of this before they look at the merits of it properly, while at the same time, their client is sending you a

---

9   An *ex parte* order is issued in the absence of one of the parties, usually to solve an urgent problem.

message which says you are going to have to spend a lot of money to get home because they are just not going to consider your claim properly. Alternatively, they may simply be trying it on.

As ever there are a variety of permutations; sometimes sensible responses come back with offers of payment.

To give one recent example, my firm wrote a pre-action letter to a bank, attaching a draft pleading accusing it of fraud and other malfeasances. We received a response from one of our larger competitors taking issue with our temerity in accusing their client of dishonesty. When we wrote back and asked whether this was the same XYZ Bank plc that had been fined millions of pounds by regulators all over the world, there was a deafening silence.

Sometimes the parties behave in a more adult way: agree what they can agree on, work out what needs to be decided and when, possibly even go so far as to agree which experts may be called in relation to areas for expert evidence (which we will deal with in Chapter 7). The savings in time and money that can be achieved through such an approach make sense on both sides.

So, the first step is to advise the other side that a claim is in prospect. Pre-action protocol letters are designed to set out clearly the basis for and the amount of the claim and elicit either a hint of the defence (in whole or in part), or payment of money, or a mixture of the two.

At this stage settlement negotiations are possible and to be encouraged. There are other things that can be sorted out to your advantage at this stage, even if litigation is necessary. There may be areas where the parties agree on some issues but not others. This is not as daft as it sounds.

Lawyers should be able to work out at least what technical issues need to be argued about, which areas of law or fact can be agreed and what needs to be sorted out and in what order. The alternative to that is a turgid day spent in court arguing over matters that could be sorted out by sensible folk in half an hour. In complex cases the cost of the 'day in court' approach can be horrendous.

Thoughts to be had at an early stage include:

- When is there going to be mediation and/or
- When is there going to be a realistic effort to effect settlement?
- When will the case be ready?
- When will both sides disclose enough to enable proper negotiations and/or settlement to happen?

There are cases where people know perfectly well that a case is going to run to a certain place and then, once all evidence has been seen, there will be a realistic attempt to settle the action or, if that is not going to happen, to take a much more realistic and informed view on how likely victory might be and on how much a decision against might cost.

Under way

The standard steps to trial in many jurisdictions include pre-action letters, pleadings, discovery, inspection, exchange of evidence (including expert reports), a stay for mediation, a pre-trial review and the setting of a date and parameters for the trial itself.

Some of these steps in Anglo-Saxon/Commonwealth jurisdictions are covered below:

1. State your case, ie the allegations of fact, the relief claimed and the legal basis for that relief ('pleadings').

2. Discovery and inspection: the gathering, filing and exchange of evidence, including a chance to see the other side's documentation.

3. The exchange and filing of witness testimony.

4. The testing of the evidence and the law at trial.

5. Judgment.

Pleadings

Different countries have different rules but the dog must see the rabbit, so they all allow the claimant to set out in written 'pleadings' what they claim and the basis for so doing, both legal and factual. The other side are then allowed to answer, rebut and counterclaim. The pleadings set the parameters for the case.

In England, pleadings are precise and detailed. In the Channel Islands, according to the rules, they are much briefer. In America they tend to be even less detailed but they all fulfil the same function, more or less.

Discovery

Discovery is the stage during the proceedings at which both parties exchange the documentary material they have which is relevant to the issues in the litigation. The discovery burden in most common law countries is an onerous one and it allows each party to obtain information from the other which may undermine or support their case.

It is important to note that a party may not purposely withhold or destroy material, whether damaging to its case or not. All material should be preserved and identified within the discovery process. Discovery both makes and breaks cases; it can be incredibly time-consuming and you and your lawyer need to discuss it at an early stage.

Discovery ordinarily involves the review by a party of the material within that party's possession, custody or power following a proper enquiry and effort in relation to such a search for material which could include letters, emails, reports, written notes, drawings, plans and photographs, etc. The material is then listed or grouped in a logical way (eg chronologically). This list is exchanged with the other side, who can ask to inspect originals in some circumstances. It is normal for the parties to also agree to provide copies of any documents requested.

More and more these days, with the increased use of and reliance upon technology, discovery will involve documents held in electronic form. As such you may need a way to search electronic databases to ensure meaningful retrieval of relevant electronic documents for review. Electronic discovery software exists and experts can, and probably should, be employed to ensure that an adequate approach is taken.

Even after the parties have exchanged discovery lists, the obligation to discover continues. If further material comes into existence and/or is found which has not been disclosed previously, consideration needs to be given to bringing this to the attention of the other side.

It is important to review the material to be discovered not only to ensure it is relevant to the pleaded cases but also to identify whether any of it should not be disclosed because it is covered by 'privilege'. This might be legal advice privilege (ie communications between a lawyer and their client seeking or giving legal advice are protected from disclosure) and/or litigation privilege (ie communications or documents coming into existence after litigation has been contemplated or begun, between a client and their lawyer and/or third parties, where the chief purpose is to collect information in relation to the litigation). Documents marked 'without prejudice' and/or that are genuine attempts to settle may also be protected from inspection and further use, although naturally the other side will know of their existence.

Confidential documents do not fall outside the ambit of discovery and should be listed and available for inspection. There may be exceptions to protect or preserve particular interests, for example trade secrets.

Ideally, when it is apparent that there may be a dispute it would be prudent to consider and attempt to locate all documentation relating to the dispute without delay. This should be retained and filed carefully. To the extent that new documents are created these should also be retained and filed carefully.

It may also be advisable to warn anyone connected with or employed on the case that documents may potentially be inspected by the other side, so care should be taken not to create embarrassing or damaging documents, should they not be covered by privilege. Other safeguards include avoiding the preparation of needless notes and minutes and ensuring documents are covered by privilege by addressing them to and/ or copying in lawyers; and/or having (eg notes and memoranda) prepared by lawyers; and routing correspondence with third parties through lawyers.

While on the face of it discovery may seem and can be an onerous obligation, it may be possible to limit the extent of discovery either by agreement or by obtaining an order from the court, particularly if discovery is likely to be disproportionately expensive.

The penalties for non-compliance with the obligations of discovery can be severe, including not just cost orders but potentially having a pleading struck out.

So far, so good. What does the smart litigant do in order to get ahead? The short answer is 'think'.

What evidence do I need to win and where is it held? What documents do I have that I need to give the other side and where are they? Have the other side disclosed to me ('discovered') the documents that I know or suspect they have? If not, can we force further discovery?

The next question is how do we resource this process? Things can go badly wrong at this stage. You can spend a lot of money to no effect if you are not careful, a point made in Chapter 1. Each situation turns on its own facts but the 80/20 rule often applies, ie 80% of the results come from 20% of the effort and pre-planning is key.

DISCOVERY COSTS

Some years ago, my firm was faced with an enormous discovery task and a client with limited funds. Paralegals in the Channel Islands can charge from £150 per hour upwards; rates for lawyers and partners may be much higher. We needed about 600 man-hours, which could have added up to £90,000 even if we used a paralegal only (and we did not have one then), so the solution was outsourced to a junior barrister on a self-employed basis.

All was done in a month, expeditiously, for £30,000. We found out later that the opposition spent £500,000 for a late and incomplete service provided by a large law firm operating the usual pyramid system (where one partner is responsible for deploying a large number of support staff).

Inspection

Discovery is one thing, inspection is another.

Inspection means reading the documents 'discovered' by the opposition and then applying them. Again, think, what evidence do I need to win? How can my team accurately and expeditiously sort the wheat from the chaff? A question to ask then is what have I not got that I should have got? Again, what does the smart litigant do to get ahead? Think.

Witness testimony

The Americans are keen on depositions, video record-ings and such like. Most countries, however, use wit-ness statements, often in affidavit form.[10] There is an art to witness statements. The first point is preparation: what does/should this witness know? The second is listening and ascertaining what the witness knows, not what the witness thinks they know or, worse, what the witness thinks you want to hear. Witness testimony should be compelling, functional and unshakeable and should be confined to first-hand knowledge and hopefully corroborated by documentation, which is one of the reasons it follows on from discovery and inspection. Truthful testimony – first-hand testimony founded on fact – is unshakeable.

Getting to trial

Nearly all judicial systems have a methodology for the trial proper and for cross-examining witnesses, ie questioning them about the evidence they have given, and for filing opening and closing submissions.

---

10   Sworn, formal documents, often using legal terminology or prepared by lawyers.

This is not a practitioner's handbook; it is designed for litigants themselves. From the litigant's point of view, involvement in the preparation for trial can be beneficial. Lawyers often work under a lot of time pressures but in an ideal world the majority of both the opening and closing submissions can be written in advance and discussed with the client. If you can ask for that to be done, it is a good discipline for all those involved. As for trial itself, if they are not familiar with the process both litigants (you) and witnesses should be tutored – not as to what to say but as to how to say it and what to expect. That way your evidence can be given clearly, sincerely and swiftly despite the unfamiliar and intimidating setting.

Watching television to find out what happens in court is probably not the best way of doing this. Going and watching a trial or, better still, attending a reputable witness familiarisation course is a prudent and sometimes game-changing preparation.

Maintenance of body, and hence mind, are important. Testifying takes a lot of mental effort so it drains the body of glucose. Lawyers, witnesses and litigants need to attend to their own nourishment. Hydration increases mental alertness, so drink water. If you take all these steps you have given yourself the best chance of success.

4

Settlement And Mediation

Settlement

A lot of this book is taken up with the realities of what is in effect warfare and is designed to help get you into a winning position before, during and, if need be, after trial. Most cases, however, do not reach trial. No one should ever count on certain victory; there are too many inherent uncertainties within the system and that is a truism everywhere. Different countries have different litigation regimes and methodologies but the principles remain valid in all circumstances.

The greatest chance of success a litigant can give themself is to prepare for a final battle and if it settles along the way, well and good. The advantage of settlement is that you know what you have agreed to, the outcome is certain; whereas if you go to trial you rely on the activities of third parties and of the decisionmakers. All decisionmakers are fallible. Some jurisdictions are highly unpredictable, not to say patently corrupt and unreliable. In a well-run, respected, mature jurisdiction competent counsel can often predict the outcome with a high degree of accuracy but even then all sorts of things can go wrong.

The cases most likely to settle are those between commercially minded litigants with good-quality advisers. Cases which involve a lot of emotion or feeling can be difficult to settle because feelings cloud judgment. Bad lawyers who misadvise their clients are a fact of life; they make settlement on rational terms very difficult indeed. As set out below, however, there are some strategies for dealing with these difficulties.

So how do you get to settlement?

Cases can settle at any time and mediation is possible at any time. However, in all jurisdictions some times are better than others to start the process, let alone achieve finality. The notorious 'settlement on the courtroom steps' is best avoided as it can be rushed and not properly thought through. In practice a lot of jurisdictions will allow the parties to adjourn an action if both sides indicate a willingness to compromise and express the view that a settlement is in sight, but courts do impose pressure and deadlines.

When?

Some jurisdictions, particularly the United Kingdom, are very keen on what are known as pre-action protocol letters, which we dealt with in Chapter 3. These are letters in which the claim is explained in detail and reference is made to how this will be proved. The idea is to explain the claim and the evidence behind it in sufficient detail to let the other side know what the claim is about and their chances of success. This is where further or partial front-end loading comes into play – the more organised you are at the start, the greater the advantage.

Defendants are also invited to lay their case out at the beginning. This not only lets both sides know what is likely to happen but is a helpful aid to settlement because at a very early stage you are seeing the other side's hand and what they will try to prove at trial; later in the process you will know how they intend to prove it. I have known many disputes disappear at an early stage because one or other party is simply advised at the outset that their chances of success are slim. In other cases the recalcitrant defendant misleads their own advisers. That can continue throughout and makes settlement very difficult.

Once the action is under way the most likely next attempt at settlement is after pleadings have closed.

In Chapter 3 I described the pleadings process in some detail. It is a process which should let both parties know what the other party's case is and to a lesser extent how it will be evidenced. Pleading styles differ between countries. Our firm thinks the United States is a bit of a shambles: their pleadings tend to be quite vague, not well particularised and then they seem to go overboard on discovery. Sometimes it is not until you start to see some evidence that you actually understand what the claim is and how the other side think they are going to win it. In any event, once you know what both sides' case is, and it has been formalised in some fashion in whatever jurisdiction you are in, effectively you can start assessing the merits. At this stage, in any event, the smart litigant is well out in front because you would already have collated the documents and assessed the merits of the claim several times, an assessment which ought to be continually revised as the evidence and allegations unfold.

All actions everywhere seem to go in stages. As the cards are turned over and evidence is exchanged, you have a better idea of the merits so it is easier to assess ways in which cases should settle. Unfortunately, the longer litigation goes on, the greater the expense and sometimes the more entrenched the parties' positions become, making settlement harder. Sadly, in many cases the cost of the litigation may be the stumbling block to settlement – all the more reason to try to advance the best position early on.

Negotiating a settlement

This is not a book about negotiation; there are lots of books about that. We all negotiate daily for all sorts of goods and services and in our relationships – probably without thinking about it. It is a game of give and take, sort of. I say 'sort of' because the game should not undermine reality.

Some lawyers say 'Let us make a downward offer (I am lazy; I have earned enough; I cannot be bothered; conventional wisdom is, etc)'. The first question you should ask yourself is 'Why make an offer?' There are lots of good reasons for making offers but it is a good starting question.

If you are the plaintiff, avoid getting into a Dutch auction.[11] A good starting point and the normal way forward is for the paying party – the defendant – to make an offer. You should then assess their offer, and you might make a counter-offer. There are various shades in relation to all of this, and different things work for different folk, but if both sides make realistic offers the parties are more likely to get to an agreed negotiating position.

PERSEVERANCE PAYS

I remember one negotiation which went on for a long time. Our headline claim was £1.3 million; the defendant's opening offer was £50,000; then it went from £50,000 to £950,000 in £50,000 increments, which was a tedious waste of time that took eleven hours. It was obvious that we had a good claim and it was equally obvious that we were 'loaded for bear' and were not going to take a daft offer. We got an acceptable settlement owing to the perseverance of our team and of the mediator (see later in this chapter). Picture how this bizarre process might have taken place in correspondence.

---

11 'Dutch' auctions supposedly start with high bids that go down; the lowest bidder wins.

Well-heeled and well-advised litigants with strong cases are just not going to go away. God loves a trier but this sort of approach really is boring, time-consuming and counterproductive.

If you are going to give a little to the other side to induce them upwards you just give them a tiny bit, so the one who is going to make the eventual biggest move up or down is normally the one who starts discounting most (or least, as the case may be).

In this case we did not move at all until the offer rose to about £750,000. We simply told them to go away and start being more realistic.

At the end of the day, we got a fair deal. It was about right, given the probability of success that we had assessed. We were in two minds whether to walk out when they started at £50,000. The mediator suggested that we just keep chipping away and it worked.

There is a huge human side to settlement. Adult professionals need to build up some form of rapport, or at least feign respect and rapport with the opposition. Even if you think your opponent is a complete numpty treat them with dignity and respect, persuade them to the table and talk to them. It is probably the best thing you can do. You may be stressed, angry and fearful;

you may have unrealistic expectations; you may need simply to be heard and dealt with like a human being; your backbone may need strengthening; but at the end of the day *you* decide on the terms of any settlement (not your lawyer, and certainly not the other side's lawyer).

Negotiating with institutions

I have been through many negotiations with institutions. They like to divide and conquer and they are also prone to negotiating, not for settlement but to test the other side, to explore pressure points and to waste the other side's resources as part of a war of attrition. They sometimes suggest talking directly, 'no lawyers involved'. They try to perceive the weakest member of your team and talk mainly to them, and you can guarantee that the institution's representative will be working from a pre-lawyered script.

Playing the other side's strategies

Even mild and quite intimidated litigants, once they are told the realities of the other side's tactics, can be quite feisty and give the other side a rather unexpected experience. At this stage you need to hold your team together, everyone pointing in the same direction, and all have an agreed set of instructions so you can play the other side at their own game. Resolution and unity are key. Litigants who are angry but not irrational, who really are due the money and who have got the staying power to negotiate till they get an acceptable settlement, tend to come out best in the negotiations.

Why settle for less?

Earlier I suggested looking at reasons for discounting. Let us look at the plaintiff's reasons for discounting (for taking less than you are due), before we look at the defendant's reasons for paying more than they offer at first:

1. The actual and hidden costs of trial – please see Chapter 6. There is always a shortfall between what you spend on the process and what you will recover from the opposition. Some countries do not allow for any costs to be recovered.

2. Unless something highly abnormal is going on, no trial team can give you more than a 70% chance of winning – that is accepted as the highest probability of winning a case which, after analysis, you rate very highly. This is

because there are always uncertainties in the process.

3. Your reputation may suffer from going to law, though sometimes this is more perceived than actual.

4. Enforcement may be risky: will you actually get paid even if you win?

5. Litigation fatigue has set in. That is a reality; people are fed up with the process by the time they get to trial, the initial anger has abated, and expense and further effort become deterrents.

6. You may have lost opportunities. You could be getting on with other work and spend your time better on other, more profitable, matters.

7. Passing of time. I may have been ripped off but life has gone on and I have learned a valuable (albeit costly) lesson.

8. The commitment to get a bigger offer than the one on the table may be too much. Results from negotiations are rarely perfect from anybody's point of view.

Time, delay, expense and uncertainty are the enemies of true justice but they are realities.

A PRACTICAL EXAMPLE

Let us draw all that together and look at a realistic equation.

If you are owed £1 million and you have spent £250,000 getting this far, with a good claim having a 60% chance of success, your 'litigation risk' is 40%. If you apply a 40% discount you would be looking at £600,000. What percentage of your costs are going to be recoverable? That is another question which we have not yet addressed in this book (see Chapter 6). Let's say another 40% would represent how much more money is required to get you to trial: £150,000. You might simply take £600,000 at that stage just to be shot of the case, plus hopefully a contribution towards your costs. All risk, stress and expenditure stops.

This is a mathematical approach. Most litigants are driven by the heart, to some extent, and disinclined to take a common-sense approach.

Realistically, from the plaintiff's point of view the equation is best looked at in dry figures. Am I likely to win? How much can I live with? Insurers, who often stand behind defendants and can be hard to move as they have a book of claims to deal with, tend to treat litigation like a bookmaker making payments based on perceived odds of success or failure. Sometimes you just have to persevere. Strongly motivated litigants with all their ducks in a row can achieve high settlements, but there are always risks.

Why would defendants pay too much?

1. The actual and hidden costs of trial.

2. The risk of a total loss at trial.

3. Reputational risk. I have seen insured professionals, eg lawyers, put their own money in, to supplement contributions by their insurers.

4. The plaintiff is impecunious or ill so there can only be a Pyrrhic victory; no good can come to the defendant even if they win.[12]

5. Litigation fatigue: money and time would be better spent on other things and the passing of time, mentioned above, can influence the defendant, too.

---

12 Conversely, an institutional defendant faced with a number of similar claims may wish to gain a public victory at whatever cost, to discourage others.

A lot of my firm's work has been for plaintiffs who were in do or die situations. Insurers, in particular, are wary of such litigants as they know they will not be able to recover anything if they win and that the cost of a full trial will be added to any eventual loss. Settlement equations for do or die clients can be fairly straightforward: you can simply tell the defendant 'Pay £x or we go to trial', as in, I need £x to go away. This tends to put the defendant on the spot.

AN IMPECUNIOUS DEFENDANT

My firm represented a professional man, a surgeon, who felt that he had been fleeced by his lawyers. His reasoning was that he only sold people operations they needed, and he presumed that lawyers do likewise. He woke up to the fact that he had been through a needlessly protracted and expensive process. He was now terminally ill, had lost the ability to work and was facing crippling bills. We went to mediation knowing that, in law, he was liable. We offered 30% of the amount due, take it or leave it: if you want to sue an ill, impecunious, self-representing client, you can. It settled, as the other side did not want the embarrassment and was unlikely to get any more. Our client kept his house.

Mediation

Mediation is now all but mandatory in some jurisdictions, at least once the case is ready for trial. Like settlement discussions mediation can happen at any time and should be encouraged to happen. Some jurisdictions are struggling with the concept at the moment but it has proved highly popular and successful in most jurisdictions where has it been introduced.

A lot has been written about mediation but it is an essentially uncomplicated process. This is a negotiation conducted in private, confidentially, by the parties with or without their advisers with the assistance of a third party or parties. Nothing said may be repeated anywhere else to anyone else, ever. No one agrees anything unless they want to and if an agreement is reached it is binding. It can settle the whole action or part(s) of the action. In practice mediators are highly effective, have a high success rate and tend to leave each side feeling mildly unhappy about the eventual outcome.

Much depends on the character orientation, knowledge, skill set and good faith, not only of the parties and of the lawyers, but also of the mediator. It also helps enormously if both sides want to do a deal.

Mediation will not work if one party is not genuine and is using mediation only as a strategy to probe the other side, to gain time and exhaust the opposition, which I have unfortunately seen on several occasions. You can get over such a strategy if you are resolute and keep going. All cases of that nature my firm has encountered involved banks. Instead of mediating to reach a deal, the first round was essentially a test of willpower, accompanied shortly after by a series of not so cleverly veiled threats. The mediators were not impressed and our side called the banks' bluff.

Why does mediation work?

1. It takes place in a low-key environment, the more low-key the better. Decisions are made by human beings; if they are relaxed, they are more likely to reach an accommodation.

2. If they want to, the parties can do a deal that is not closely connected with the legal battle. Sometimes a simple apology or explanation takes the heat out. The parties may even patch things up and go back into business together.

3. The parties can talk to each other directly; sometimes that is a good idea. Likewise, the

lawyers can talk directly to each other and sometimes that too is a good idea. Moreover, if the opposition refuse a lawyer-to-lawyer meeting organised in a relaxed environment to sort out any disputes as to what the law means you know that they are flying a kite.

4. The parties may differ on the core facts. Outside the litigation arena they can explore what did or did not really happen and reach a reasonable, non-binding consensus for settlement purposes.

5. Lawyer-to-lawyer contact can allow the ritualised position to be left aside: both sides' advisers can look at the most likely result if you go to court.

6. Within reason, parties can do and say what they want. No deal is done until it is all over and an agreement has been signed. The mediator will apply pressure to get a deal done. Rather than lose a deal the mediator might send the parties away for months at a time to reflect and, possibly, talk to each other and try again. Meanwhile, the parties may look at the facts again and exchange documents and thoughts. The possibilities are endless.

7. In some scenarios the parties can agree outline
    terms and conditions for a deal with the detail
    and amount to be filled in later. This is to be
    encouraged; everyone then knows that a deal is
    in prospect.

MEDIATION

I remember one mediation where the parties were
millions of pounds apart. At mediation we drew up a
template for what a deal might look like. It took six
more months to sort out the amounts, but we did it.

Mediators themselves

What of the mediator him- or herself? They are there
to kill the litigation, no two ways about it. Who gets
what is not their problem. They are there to facilitate
a deal, almost any deal; to them a settlement, almost
any settlement, is a win. Some pass no judgment and
express no opinion at all, but I have also seen the exact
opposite, where the mediators rolled up their sleeves
and examined the detail. In one difficult case the litigant was timid and depressed, the other side were
shamelessly unpleasant, the mediator gently teased

more facts out of the litigant than we had and we achieved a fair settlement.

In my experience there are, in effect, two types of mediation: straight or directed. Ordinary (or straight) mediation means simply that the mediator will facilitate a settlement, often without ever expressing a view on the merits or even the sum sought, and this approach works best if the mediator nudges the parties towards reality. Conversely, in a directed mediation the mediator will express views and opinions. They are not binding but the parties will learn what a third party makes of the opposing claims.

Mediators themselves can be divided between specialists and generalists:

1. The mediator who is a jack of all trades tends to express no views at all but pushes the parties' emotional buttons to achieve a deal, by using their skills of diplomacy; and

2. the mediator who is informed in the area the litigation relates to, while ordinarily not expressing a view *per se*, assists the parties to reach a sensible, fact- and logic-based accommodation, often greatly facilitated by their specialised knowledge.

I have found the second sort more effective; I think they give better value and produce fairer outcomes. If they know the subject matter and have experience in the area, they can suggest that the parties have a good look at the strengths and weaknesses surrounding the areas of the case. While it is unlikely that a generalist mediator will express a view on the merits, if the mediator knows the area well they can pose awkward questions in private and identify some real issues. These may be matters touched on by the litigants or lawyers but it may be more meaningfully done by a mediator. This can be difficult territory for a mediator so many avoid it, preferring to maintain a friendly façade of complete neutrality.

There is also 'shuttle-style' mediation: repetitive rounds of subtle diplomacy, endlessly conveying messages or offers from one side to the other. It can work but I have seen it fail several times. It requires patience and the mediator doing their utmost, with a genuine appetite for settlement. In one case we dealt with involving a professional partnership, the 'shuttler' spent hours trying to get one of the parties to do a deal with an outgoing partner. It was simply not going to fly as the plaintiff had offered to pay what was due. The rest of the case was nonsensical: the plaintiff was not going to pay more than the amount at issue, whatever the mediator did. A bit of common sense and some views from the mediator could have seen us all go home a lot earlier with a deal.

The worst type of mediators mercilessly play the person rather than the issue, preying on the weaker party until an accommodation is achieved, ultimately by psychological pressure, so the deal may have little or no connection with merit. If the mediator is spending a disproportionate amount of time in close contact with you, this may not be a good sign. Lay down some boundaries; do not be pressured into a deal unrelated to the merits of the claim. I remember an intimidated litigant opposed by a ruthless partnership of lawyers. She had a blank letter law contract on her side,[13] but her advisers allowed the mediator to sit next to her, and she caved in. It was a bad outcome.

The better mediators, in my view, look at the issues and help establish common ground. A knowledgeable, personable mediator coming from a successful career in the relevant industry gets the respect of both sides.

Directed mediations work when the mediator gives a clear quasi-judicial steer to how they see the case

---

13   An unambiguous, legally enforceable contract.

being concluded at trial (based on the information they have). The mediator issues a non-binding 'indicative determination', on which the parties can comment, or accept or reject; it cuts through the blather and posturing. Directed mediations work particularly well in matrimonial cases. It is the best and most effective methodology for settling divorce cases I have yet encountered, and I would like to see it used outside the family arena. In England, rules of court provide for Financial Dispute Resolutions (FDR), a type of directed mediation that has proved popular and effective. That is not the case for all countries, but in those countries it may nevertheless be possible for the parties to simply agree that a qualified judge conduct the mediation and give a judicial steer. The judge will read the case papers, listen to the parties and then say, if this case were before me I would be thinking along the following lines; would you like to do a deal?

Winning mediation strategies in a nutshell

1. Be organised – the smart litigant already is.

2. Give thought to the identity of the mediator, their skill set and their background.

3. Have a clear idea of the parameters of settlement and what is/is not acceptable.

4. Stick to your guns but be realistic from the off.

5. Be polite and establish, if possible, rapport and mutual respect – if not possible, be practical: fake it until you make it.

6. Listen to the other side; understand where they are coming from, if for no other reason than understanding the nature of the beast.

7. Never give the mediator your bottom line and do not tell them anything you do not want the other side to know. Better safe than sorry.

8. Remember the mediator is not your friend; (s)he is there to settle the litigation, which is a win for the mediator even if it is a loss for the litigant.

9. Never be afraid to break off or come back another day.

10. Do not do a deal for the sake of it.

5
Fraud

In this chapter, the first of a number dealing with specific topics, we look at what fraud is, how the smart litigant spots a fraudster and what you can do about it.

Fraud has a major negative impact on all economies globally, as do bribery and corruption. From an individual's point of view and from the point of view of the honest corporate, this is a major problem. All of us have lost money and opportunities as a result of the dishonest actions of others, normally more than one individual acting in concert with one or more other people who are willing participants, or who have been manipulated into complying, or who do not care about the consequences of their actions.

Frauds range from the mundane – for example, fraudulently obtaining credit or goods – to racketeering involving teams of people, with considerable investment and sophistication being deployed by the fraudsters, through to courses of consistently dishonest conduct by well-known institutions who remunerate and incentivise staff for their success in fleecing customers.

We deal later in this book with suing institutions of this kind. However, the public trust banks and other major institutions, and where that trust is misplaced law enforcement and regulators levy swingeing fines. Think of Lloyds and its famous black horse, 'by your side' – fined £45.5 million in June 2019 for channelling client money into lavish holidays and sex parties.

The effects on individuals and small to medium-sized businesses can be terminal, anything from loss of profits to bankruptcy, divorce, illness and death. Conventional law enforcement is more often than not completely ineffective to deter and detect, let alone catch, punish and gain recompense. The position is even worse in relation to cybercrimes, which are often run with great sophistication from lawless countries, for example, parts of Eastern Europe, Nigeria and the Philippines.

In England, a 'developed world' country, you are very much on your own. Let us look at a simpler and more blatant crime with equally devastating effects, burglary. It is invasive, soul-destroying and potentially highly dangerous. In England and Wales, both 'developed' countries, it is not so much a plague as a way of life; law enforcement is not funded nor motivated to assist, let alone deter. There were 650,000 burglaries in 2016/17, per the Office for National Statistics. Now compare this with the 3,241,000 instances of fraud in 2016/17 in England and Wales, of which 102,000 were advanced fee frauds. According to Scotland Yard the clear-up rate, ie conviction rate, is about 5%.[14] Detection and deterrence are being passed to private suppliers, from private investigators to private security firms to lawyers and accountants.

Before looking at what you can do about fraud let us look into the mind of the fraudster. These are people intentionally or recklessly trying to enrich themselves at the expense of others. They do not care about what is done to third parties; rarely do they regret what they have done.

For the better part of the public this is both shocking and inexplicable: why do people behave like this?

---

14   Data on judicial and non-judicial outcomes from instances of fraud are available at www.actionfraud.police.uk/data.

Either they calmly weigh up the consequences, which is what big corporates do, or (quite often) they are psychopaths.

The definition of a psychopath is perhaps not what you would expect. The word conjures up thoughts of violent crime, but in fact not all psychopaths are violent or psychotic. A psychopath can be defined as 'a person with an antisocial personality disorder, manifested in aggressive, perverted, criminal, or behaviour without empathy or remorse'.[15] Often highly intelligent and prone to manipulating others, psychopaths can appear 'normal' but are lacking in some human emotions such as guilt or shame. It is important to note that not all psychopaths are serial killers.

Psychopathy is a dysfunctional psyche, devoid of the normal balancing mechanisms which hold the negative emotions within human beings in check, namely shame, fear of retribution, fear of exposure, guilt and remorse.

A clinical trial, which we are told was lawfully carried out, found that an ordinary member of society, if wired up to a pair of electrodes and told that they will be given an electric shock in five minutes time, will

---

15   See www.urbandictionary.com/define.php?term=psychopath.

immediately become apprehensive, start sweating and become distressed. Psychopaths start to worry about ten seconds before the jolt.[16] This is a very striking aid to explaining how and why they manage to keep several balls in the air for so long and why they so often react with indifference when steps are taken to hold them to account.

In an even more striking statistic, valid studies estimate the number of board members/chairmen having psychopathic tendencies at about 25%.[17] Perhaps that explains the callousness and dishonesty exhibited by so many large organisations.

There are a lot of definitions and information available on psychopaths, both online and in book form. Robert D Hare's books *Snakes in Suits* and *Without Conscience* are dated but valid reference books.[18]

---

16 Hare, R.D. (1965). 'Psychopathy, fear arousal and anticipated pain', *Psychological Reports*, 16(2), pp. 499–502. doi: 10.2466/https://journals.sagepub.com/doi/10.2466/pr0.1965.16.2.499.

17 Fritzon, K. & Bailey, C. & Croom, S. & Brooks, N. (2016). 'Problem personalities in the workplace: Development of the corporate personality inventory'. www.taylorfrancis.com/chapters/edit/10.1201/9781315317045-20.

18 Hare, R.D. *Snakes in Suits* (London: HarperCollins, 2006); Hare, R.D. *Without Conscience* (New York: Guilford Publications, 1999).

It is helpful to look at some examples at how this plays out in public. Perhaps my firm (Sinels) has become so cynical as a result of repeatedly dealing with fraudsters that our radars are too finely tuned; however, we and many others have met the following behaviours:

1. *Opulence and ostentation.* Handbags, watches, jewellery, clothes. Designer clothing is all very well in moderation but in excess it points to skewed values. The male fraudster typically has many watches, £1,000 shirts, mink-lined boots, jeans that cost £500 etc, and his wife or girlfriend may have hundreds, if not thousands, of pairs of shoes, expensive handbags and related.

2. *Excessive consumption of food.* A significant percentage of fraudsters appear above average weight or morbidly obese. I have occasionally warned local restaurants about customers that I accurately predicted were not on the straight and narrow but were obtaining big lines of credit for food and drink.

3. *Ostentatious speech.* Be wary of people who speak loudly, using overly rounded vowels in restaurants and public places, let alone in private.

4. *Expensive 'toys'*. Luxury cars, expensive knick-knacks, £6,000 phones, helicopters etc are often another tell-tale sign, especially if not really needed.

5. *False strokes*. Allow me to do this for you, bending over backwards, how can I help? etc, showing excessive gratification if you agree, over-politeness followed by a proposition which is too good to be true. Extending it outside the social arena, fraudsters will often obtain credit by building up a false positive trading record, for example by buying and selling a series of high-end motor cars on credit. The credit company has a perfectly operated account until the last transaction.

6. *Advance fee frauds are all the same*. A glittering financial opportunity is promised, you just have to pay a little money up front... If it is too good to be true, it is probably not true. A staggering number of sophisticated, worldly-wise business-people fall for what with hindsight were obvious scams. Remember the current statistics on advance fee frauds?

7. *How many of us have been short-changed on a final account?* There are household names who

see this as a legitimate business tool. In the construction industry this is rife. It is nasty, dishonest behaviour, leaving honest contractors broken, particularly the smaller ones. Non-payment of smaller businesses by larger ones conducted as a policy is dishonesty personified.

8. *Correspondence and actions which delay and obfuscate; promises and frequent failures to answer questions.* My firm has seen so many compositions of this nature that the alarm bells have normally gone off by the end of the second paragraph.

RUSSELL KING

Russell King was convicted of fraud in Jersey in 2019. He showed many of the traits listed above. As a result of multiple applications for credit for cars, he had a good credit rating. Perhaps somebody should have twigged to the fact that he had so many cars that he was unlikely to use, and that given his considerable size was unlikely to find driving a sports car a comfortable experience. What was he doing with so many of them?

He and his business partner also owned a small helicopter, a vanity acquisition, coupled with

handmade monogrammed shirts and related
ostentatious items.[19]

What is fraud?

Our own definition comes from following the money:
all frauds involve benefits flowing one way for little
or no consideration.

Black's Law Dictionary defines fraud as follows:

- 'knowing' or 'reckless misrepresentation', or a
  'concealment of material fact' intended to 'induce
  another to act to his or her detriment'

- a deal resulting from an 'unconscientious use
  of the power arising out of the parties' relative
  positions'

- in terms of property deals, a 'transfer of property
  for little or no consideration' that is designed to
  put that property out of reach of any creditors.[20]

---

19 In 2011, the BBC's *Panorama* current affairs programme showed a
    documentary on King called 'The Trillion Dollar Con-Man'.
20 Bryan Garner, ed., *Black's Law Dictionary*, eighth edition (2004), s.v.,
    'fraud.'

However it is defined, fraud is the act of obtaining benefit without concomitant risk or adequate payment, or by avoiding an obligation. What it always comes down to, and that is the point of it, is to get something for little or (preferably) nothing, or to avoid paying for something they have already had.

Perhaps surprisingly, I find that ordinary people are often better than professionals at spotting fraud. They know when they have been defrauded, although sometimes it takes a little time for the enormity of it to set in. However, the 'F' word, as it is sometimes known, should not be misused; it has to be deployed with caution. There are consequences – positive and negative – for using it.

For a lawyer or accountant, in many countries the rules in relation to pleading fraud are restrictive. The practitioner is expected not to make the allegation unless they have clear instructions to do so and reasonably credible evidence exists that establishes an arguable case of fraud.

You can guarantee that the most dishonest and unscrupulous fraudsters are likely to be the ones who complain loudest about being accused, and about their accusers' legal advisers. For example, one ringleader went on to complain about the actions of the Advocate for the plaintiff, the independent supervising Advocate (Jersey legal offices) and the IT experts involved. A constant theme was that he had done nothing wrong.

Here is an extract from the ringleader's own correspondence, part of a transcript of a conversation between two conspirators discussing another member of the gang (A) who was still working for the victim (C):

'Much as expected! He [C] will now have to rely on [A] to rebuild his company if that is his intention. A few months of losses should put a stop to that plus his inability to recruit in Jersey. His best bet is to relaunch in Dubai! It may be that he will confront you so I hope you have got a good cover story. You can blame ▮▮▮▮▮▮▮▮, that mysterious Far East Investment Company with Shipping and Trading connections. [A] is clearly going to take the brunt of his anger! Hopefully he will lose his temper which will give [A] a way out.'

'A' later sent the following message:

'...[B]oth [B] and I are of the opinion that once the dust has settled and the reality of his loss of revenue becomes apparent in the face of the significant costs of ███████ in Jersey, [C] will retract the business to Dubai and relaunch from there. There is no real reason for him to confront me, but I'm not worried if he does – a business case and opportunity was placed at my feet and I decided to pick it up, thanks to your support.'

There was no hint of contrition by any of the defendants, and there were many of them. This is just how they thought you should do business. Another surprising fact of fraud is that it is infectious: employees will decide *en masse* to steal from an employer or uplift their erstwhile employer's business. To them this way is simply how you do business.

The disadvantage of alleging fraud

Alleging fraud has a number of potential drawbacks:

1. It is hard to prove, harder than breach of contract, which is often the alternative.

2. Judges discourage the misuse of the 'F' word – both by leaning on counsel and by being

reluctant to find it proven without really good, clear evidence.

3. If you allege fraud but fail, then you may have prejudiced a perfectly good case that could have been brought home as a breach of contract or similar.

4. In some jurisdictions costs might be awarded against a party for alleging dishonesty and then failing.

5. You may win your case but end up paying the fraudster's costs.

6. Sometimes there is an innocent explanation or a confused position, with one side not knowing what the other was doing.

7. Not all the participants may have the same level of culpability: bit-part players should not have their lives turned upside down needlessly. I have seen that too often. America seems to be a little different as putting on a lot of pressure in order to turn witnesses seems to be accepted there.

Alleging fraud to the authorities is not a straightforward equation. It depends on where you are and on the circumstances. Often they do nothing and you are kept wholly in the dark about the process. Additionally, fines are paid, not to the victims but to the government.

The criminal process can override the civil process, which is then 'stayed' indefinitely, a fraudster can rarely be criticised for spending their money on defence or prevented from doing so, and if they are jailed they may not then be able to repay what they have stolen.

In some jurisdictions the criminal prosecutor will keep the claimant/victim at arm's length. In other jurisdictions the victim gets to be included in the process with documents and information being shared in real time. Going to the authorities is rarely a cure for all ills but it has its place.

The advantages of alleging fraud and proving it

Having looked at some of the disadvantages of alleging fraud, which include an increased risk in countries with adverse costs regimes and a higher evidential burden, we can look at the advantages of successfully proving fraud.

1. *Fraud unravels all.* Once fraud is found it vitiates (ie destroys the validity of) all judgments, contracts and related transactions whatsoever. That is an enormous consequence.

2. *Judicial assistance:*

   – Each country is different but, as a rule of thumb, properly alleging and proving fraud has advantages. Most courts generally like to assist victims of fraud, particularly in obvious cases, it gives the judge a 'feel good' moment and reflects well on the state or county involved.

   – Some less salubrious, particularly offshore, jurisdictions adopt or have adopted the opposite approach, eg no frauds happen here therefore we are going to punish you for alleging it.

3. *Prescription.* Successfully alleging fraud may extend the period within which action can be taken, either by setting aside the time limit entirely, or by extending it, or by starting the clock from the discovery of the fraud, not the occurrence of the fraud itself. That is particularly common where some or all of the fraudster's actions are taken to cover their tracks or, as we

have seen above, to cause so much damage that
their victim is unable to fund pursuit.

4. *Void and voidable.* In some circumstances,
   contracts can be vitiated by fraud, enabling
   the other party to step away from the contract.
   Until they elect to do so the contract still exists.
   A contract vitiated by fraud can be void *ab
   initio*, treated as never being made and never
   enforceable. Fraudulent conduct is a factor that
   can materially impact on this equation. In many
   respects it can be advantageous for one party
   to prove fraud so as to vitiate the contract *ab
   initio* rather than trying to reset the clock later
   on: this can mean that in law there was never an
   obligation to perform at all.

5. *Damages:*

   – The damages to be awarded may be increased
     as a result of precedent or statute. At the
     extreme end of the scale is the US RICO
     statute (Racketeer-Influenced and Corrupt
     Organizations Act), which allows the plaintiff
     in a civil action to recover up to treble the
     amount of damages actually incurred or
     ordinarily available as compensation. This
     statute was brought in to deal with the Mafia,

primarily to empower law enforcement, but it has had the consequence of helping plaintiffs in civil suits. This can be highly beneficial.

 - Further down the scale, the judge may be sympathetic on the effect of the fraud, eg award increased damages, look more sympathetically at how foreseeable the fraud was. Foreseeability can be a big factor in damages calculation. Was the damage suffered foreseeable or not? Once the fraudster has been successfully convicted then the foreseeability test can get a lot easier.

6. *Injunctions, civil search-and-seizure orders:*

 - As ever, each country has its own regime. Although these orders are not restricted to fraud cases, they are nearly always granted where some form of actual or anticipated dishonesty is at issue, such as destruction of evidence or dissipation of assets in anticipation of judgment.

 - The orders available range from injunctions, which prevent things being done (for example the movement of goods and money), through to requiring goods or money to be handed over. Increasingly, these days, documents and

RESTITUTION AND HOW TO OBTAIN IT

information are requested, for safe keeping or
for examination.

- These are at the more extreme end of the scale
  because these orders can be overly intrusive.
  A starting point for obtaining the order is
  showing that the defendant is not likely
  to comply with court orders and will take
  action to destroy evidence or judgment proof
  themselves.

- *In extremis* orders can be granted to allow the
  search for information and its removal and
  duplication on the spot.

- In truly extreme cases the courts will
  prevent movement not only of goods and
  money but of people. This can be quite
  a feature of sharia-law countries where
  preventing movement is seen as a way of
  extracting money and/or security for a
  claim. In some parts of the Middle East the
  threshold can be quite low. In Anglo-Saxon/
  Commonwealth jurisdictions the courts
  are loath to make orders of that kind but
  in certain circumstances will peremptorily
  remove a passport from a flight risk where

circumstances warrant; however, very cogent evidence is needed.

- These are all at the heavy end of the permissibility and obtainability scale; this is perhaps just as well. If they were available day-to-day it would make inroads into people's rights to privacy. However, they are sometimes necessary, and they are most often available as a consequence of fraud and dishonest conduct.

7. *Timetabling*. Again, frauds, particularly those which produce a slew of urgent applications, can cause the court to engage proactively and sympathetically with the claimant to get them the relief that they need, before the matter becomes a procedural morass of the type that all fraudsters love and encourage. In the mind of the beast, delay is always a good thing.

8. *Enforcement against fraudsters:*

- A fraudster has never paid any money or performed an obligation until you actually have it in your hand, ie the money has cleared (not just appeared as a credit), all the documents have been produced and they have been examined to make sure that they are genuine.

– Never get sucked into relaxing an order on the basis of a promise. Promises are cheap and are often broken. Either you have had money or the security has actually been placed, to your absolute satisfaction, in the right place; or it does not exist.

– The same *modus operandi* applies to orders for meeting time limits. That is why, if you give an extension to a fraudster in relation to compliance with anything, it should always be done on the basis that, now, today, you will not take action for contempt, but you have not waived your right to do so.

There are as many stories about fraud and fraudsters as there are lawyers in this specialised field but the story below is quite illuminating; it shows the system working at its best, to the advantage to the defrauded.

A TRUE STORY

Ms S was the client of a trust company. Unfortunately, she actually had more control of the assets within the structure day-to-day than did the trustee. She and the trustee decided they wanted to part ways. The trustee had outstanding bills going back many years for about £150,000 and asked her to pay £50,000, after which it would hand over everything that she wanted, including control of the structure, and that would be the end of the matter.

After a number of delays and the production of what could best be called Bollywood defences, including, at the last minute, suddenly alleging that the trustee had lost some £10 million more than ten years earlier but that Ms S had forgotten about it until now, she agreed that the matter of the outstanding invoices could go to arbitration. She insisted that there be one arbitrator, whose decision would be final and binding. The trustee, who was fed up with the matter, agreed.

The trustee was quite happy to hand over all Ms S's other assets to her and, in effect, to dismantle her structure, provided only that it received security while awaiting the outcome of the arbitration. Security was in the form of the shares in an offshore company which owned a valuable property.

The share certificates were lodged with a reputable firm of local lawyers by Ms S.

The arbitration ruled that she had to pay most of the invoices as drawn plus the trustee's costs and of course she had to absorb her own. She then appealed against this ruling – an order made by a joint expert that she had agreed was unappealable – and failed. Her own costs multiplied several times, by introducing other firms of lawyers to act for other family members alleging that the trustee had lost other, non-existent amounts of money.

At this stage and upon receipt of the final judgment, Ms S was asked to pay what she owed under the court direction but nothing was forthcoming.

Fresh property searches were then undertaken, only to discover that the property put up as security pending the adjudication was now recorded at the Land Registry as being owned by someone else. Fearing that this name was an alias for Ms S or a family member, we sent a retired policeman to visit the property early one morning, only to discover that the owner was exactly who he and the Land Registry said he was.

What we discovered after some examination was that Ms S had forged documents to allow her to sell the property. She was in breach of any number of court orders and was acting in contempt of court. An interesting point to note along the way is that the English Land Registry take no responsibility for actions of this nature and there is no compensation scheme.

The trustee obtained injunctions; banks were made to disclose information and documentation; eventually security was obtained over a bank account. Ms S, colourful to the last, had some interesting exchanges with the process servers. They served three sets of documents on her in one day, the first at 11.00am and the second at 2.00pm and then at 4.00pm. When asked on the second occasion whether or not she was the same Ms S who had been served that morning by the same process server, she replied 'No'.

Ms S's whereabouts then became something of an issue and we had to put her under surveillance.

Ms S was forced to attend court to answer a contempt charge, and her passport was removed pending finalisation of the proceedings. Along the way she produced a sickness certificate designed to procure a delay, so we examined the *bona fides* of the doctor who signed it and he turned out to be a former partner.

All matters ended successfully for the trustee. Ms S was fined £30,000 for contempt and ordered to pay further sets of costs. The trustee was awarded the maximum possible contribution towards its costs available in law, including the cost of injunctive relief in two different countries, and the whole of its arbitration award. We worked out that Ms S's liability, which could have been resolved for £50,000, cost her over £1 million. The trustee and its advisers were perfectly correct to allege fraud, not from the start but from the moment that they realised that the property had been sold in breach of the agreed orders using forged documentation.

CONCLUSIONS

- It can help to have been defrauded, as your remedies and damages are enhanced.

- However, fraud is an allegation to be made with care.

- Each case will depend on the facts.

- Each jurisdiction has its own laws and rules specific to allegations of fraud.

- If you have been defrauded, law enforcement is not a cure-all; it may be counterproductive, it may, however, have its place.

6

How To Finance
Your Litigation

This is a chapter about how to identify and deal with both the hidden and the direct costs of litigation. The potential cost can be a determining factor as to whether or not to litigate at all, and if so how long to carry on for.

Internal costs

There are two types of cost, external and internal. Many litigants forget to even think about the internal costs. The internal costs themselves come in two forms.

Depending on the nature of the case, you and your witnesses will suffer varying levels of stress and anxiety, which will impact on your ability to function at home and in the office. Also, there is the sheer amount of time involved, a big factor for professional firms who, in effect, sell time.

A good legal team can help in a number of ways, as explained below, but the human costs also need to be managed by and with the help of peers, friends, family and, *in extremis*, counsellors.

Litigation is stressful and it needs to be flagged as being stressful and managed accordingly. The same human equation can apply to both witnesses and potential witnesses. Witnesses, whether they are parties to the litigation or not, can benefit enormously from witness familiarisation courses. My firm had a client who was facing a hostile time in the witness box and no amount of explaining to him the process allayed his trepidation. A full day on a properly run witness familiarisation course gave him a great deal of peace of mind. These courses are invaluable for first-time litigants and first-time witnesses. In my experience they are run competently and ethically. The process is explained but the witness is not coerced to give evidence a particular way; that is unethical and in some countries unhelpful.

The other internal cost is time and disruption. In an organisation everybody's time has a value so the less time anybody spends on the litigation the better. Some time will inevitably have to be spent but it can and should be managed. There are some trade-offs: administrative tasks that can be completed more cheaply internally than externally, for example collating documentation and related. Communication with your lawyers and a litigation plan can help enormously.

What helps with bigger cases is a liaison point between the legal team and the person or organisation running the litigation.

Tips for saving time and money

1. *Witness proofs.* Take depositions early on, at the start instead of later. Going around in circles and back and forth later in the case is expensive. Having the depositions you need also helps stop the case tying itself in knots later, and needing multiple amendments. This process will also help identify quite quickly where both strengths and weaknesses exist in the case.

2. Get *all the relevant documents* together at the start. We deal in Chapter 3 with discovery but

at the start identify the sources of relevant documentation and collate it; hours of stress and expense can be saved by doing that.

3. Insist on *a formal litigation plan* at the outset: what money and input (ie information) is needed and when? Much of litigation is like a set-piece, rule-driven chess game, so it should be possible to plan in advance. The unexpected can and frequently does happen but that is no excuse for not making the best plan possible in advance.

4. Agree *the allocation of tasks* with the lawyers, gain guidance as to how the evidence-gathering tasks can be best achieved.

5. Appoint one person to *liaise with the legal team* and ask for *monthly briefings and progress reports*. These might be very brief or in other cases slightly more detailed, but they should exist. Then you can see what you are paying for and where you are going. If you do not get a breakdown or clear narrative explaining how the fees are being charged then this should be demanded and it is important to review these charges to understand what is being done, how expensive things are and whether the charges are fair and reasonable.

6. *Best estimated cost to trial* should be requested
   (ie an estimate of what the trail will cost). It is
   inherently difficult to predict the costs but a
   best guess, whether highly qualified or not, will
   still be useful, normally. Some jurisdictions may
   require, in the early stages, budgets/estimates to
   be exchanged with the other side.

INTERNAL COSTS

Some years ago, my firm sued a large, bank-owned
trustee for fraud. They made a number of errors
in the course of the litigation. They had to redo
discovery in the middle of the trial because they
had not done it properly the first time, which led to
a lot of judicial criticism. They had clearly failed to
take a statement from their witness in advance to
check what the witness could and would say at trial
and found themselves having to learn that on their
feet in the courtroom. Two large teams of lawyers
represented the trustee, some from London and
some local, but they were constantly caught on the
back foot, notably when an early attempt to derail
the case failed.

One thing that emerged during trial was that,
although it was a big organisation, the trustee's
profits were adversely affected not only by the
external costs of the litigation (one of their lawyers

105

was charging at least three times what we were) but by the paralysis, disruption and loss of time to people inside the organisation. Personally, I thought they should have sacked their lawyers. We would have settled for much less than we received at trial and they would have avoided being on the end of a long, well-reasoned finding of fraud, much publicised in legal and financial circles. We know all this because, owing to a twist in the litigation, we got hold of their accounts.

External costs

Litigation at any level uses lawyers, specialist counsel (in some jurisdictions), forensic and intelligence support and expert witnesses. Many of these costs are foreseeable and may be estimated.

One of the biggest areas of dispute, difficulty and sometimes dismay tends to relate to legal fees *per se*.

Start by knowing the nature of the beast. Lawyers in many countries work on an hourly rate. These vary significantly in themselves. In London you can pay £300–£1,000 per hour, but the biggest variations come with the use and misuse of the pyramid system internally within large firms of solicitors (see below) and as a result of counsel making a meal of it at £700 per hour or more.

Where hours are being sold (and in the big firms the emphasis is very much on selling hours), to make the maximum amount of money one partner will have, for example, six people reporting to him and their income attributed to him. He is the one who makes the profit so once you have that pyramid structure in place, the partner needs to feed the machine.

Watch out for swish offices with atriums and firms where every email, however trivial, is copied to multiple fee earners. You are unlikely to be getting good value. This is so well known in some circles that one extremely good firm of lawyers I know deliberately uses the most washed-out, scruffy meeting room you can imagine, to show that they are not that kind of lawyer.

With complex litigation you will need to liaise with one or more people at the law firm who are able to make decisions. In fairness to lawyers there is a need for continuity and sanity checks. Difficult decisions are sometimes best made by two heads rather than one.

You are more likely to receive value and responsiveness from smaller, specialised law firms or, if you use a large law firm, by dealing with one partner and one fee earner, and insisting on a tight control of costs.

My firm has a relatively flat structure but we are not Pound World; we produce quality products and our hourly rates are similar to a lot of other local law firms. We have had some surprising results when we compare our charges to those of other firms and I give some examples below.

The first was in a £10 to £15 million case. We needed to deal with a relatively straightforward summons by the other side, seeking to strike out parts of a pleading with some complex technical and legal points involved – our estimate for this, which was going to take half a day in court, was around £15,000. The other side turned up hoping to win and get a summary assessment of their costs, with a bill of £55,000. The reason for that was sitting in the room: one partner, two assistants and an imported QC. We fielded one partner and one assistant.

In a trial of some complexity against a decision by the JFSC (the financial services regulator in Jersey), we had a four-day, paper-heavy trial with a number of complexities both legal and factual. Our costs for the trial itself were £90,000. The other side's were over £400,000. This was a mid-range firm with comparable hourly rates to ourselves; the difference was in the number of people they used and the extraordinarily long hours that they worked: no one in our firm managed to exhibit that much stamina. We attended court with one partner and one assistant, they attended regularly with three lawyers, as well as support from two people from the JFSC. Additionally, that firm was employing, as fee earners, people whose qualifications were unknown and one or more who appeared to be related to one of the principals. We also noted that one particular fee earner, who was being charged out at £150 per hour, had no qualifications whatsoever. Looking at the equation from the other firm's point of view, they had a £30,000 employee but were looking to and able to gain 1,200 chargeable hours at £150 per hour, ie £180,000 per year in chargeable fees.

The third example related to a mediation with the same firm that we mentioned in the first example above. By this stage the proceedings were at an advanced stage, the pleadings had closed and discovery was about to start. It was a £10 million claim against a clearing bank. As an aid to settlement the mediator asked us what we estimated our costs might reach by the end of the trial if it went that far. We said realistically, including expert witnesses, a maximum of £400,000. The other firm, deadpan, said £2.5 million, at which stage we pointed out that if they wanted to spend money like that they could but it was never going to be a liability for our side; even if we lost, it would be reduced substantially in 'taxing' (see Chapter 2). However, that is the level of bills that the larger firm was expecting to charge their corporate client.

Another time, I was told by somebody who used to work at that particular corporation that they had a hands-off policy – once it went to legal, they did not control the bills. Good work for some but how could you expect to see a good return at the end of the day?

Another point relative to value for money is a law firm's culture. If they are pushing fee earners to charge out 2,000 hours a year (some American law firms do – this is nearly eight hours a day, every working day), or even 1,500 hours (nearly six hours a day), then those hours have to be spent somewhere. Bear in mind that training, any marketing or internal admin work, and general keeping up to date, which is pretty important in a law firm, need to be done on top of these chargeable hours. You can see that over-ambitious charging targets create incentives to dump and churn.

My firm often act for plaintiffs facing institutions. On the basis of experience, we can predict that they are spending more than our clients, sometimes three or more times more. This is quite a good impetus for the other side to settle.

Raising the money

You need to cover your own costs and the opposition's too (if the case goes wrong and if you are bringing it in a jurisdiction that awards costs against the losing party). By now these should be open to some form of estimation although, as we have seen from the examples above, estimating the other side's costs on any rational basis is sometimes all but impossible.

This business of having to work out what it might cost if it goes wrong is hard, and one way of looking at it is to say, well, I have got my side's costs under control, I have a reasonable estimate, I can rely, to some extent at least, on the judicial system 'taxing' (see Chapter 2) the other side's bills to a 'realistic' level. Some jurisdictions insist on all parties exchanging budgets at an early stage.

The possibility of adverse costs orders do deter some people from litigating. Other litigants, by choice or by necessity, work on the do or die principle: even if it all goes horribly wrong, well, life has already gone wrong and they may not have much left if they do nothing.

Sources of funding

1. *Your own assets* and revenue either from those assets, your own business(es) or friends and family.

2. *Sell the claim.*

   – In some countries you can sell claims to organisations that make a business of fighting for a settlement. Some of the bigger operators will also buy debts. Debts are what you owe other people, a claim is what you need to prove in order for someone to owe you a debt. This is not possible in all countries (again, I am trying to cover a broad spectrum of the litigation world).

   – The bigger operations can be quite flexible: in large claims some may finance the litigant to continue their business (or at least eat) until the end of the trial.

- This approach is very expensive, because on completion the purchaser is going to want to take a big slice of the award. However, it may be the only option left. This can be a devastatingly effective approach where the litigant has gone bankrupt, or is close to it, as a result of fraud perpetrated by someone else.

3. *Crowdfunding.* My firm has not tried it but it is possible. There is no reason why you could not crowdfund a claim, especially if it is on a point of public interest, ie a test case on a novel point with wide applicability.

4. *Class actions.* Have other people suffered the same wrong, perpetrated by the same person(s) or class of people? This is often the case in mis-selling cases. Actions against big corporations/ pharmaceutical companies and the like can attract any number of fellow litigants who all have essentially the same case, on the same or similar facts. This brings the costs per participant down but can lead to complications on who gets what share of an eventual award because the other side will do their best to sow dissent.

5. *A small group of litigants?* If one specialist law
   firm in an area handles a particular type of
   claim and you have allied problems, even
   against different defendants, it is possible that
   your lawyers might be prepared to pool their
   knowledge and resources with that other firm.
   My firm has done this: parts of the work were
   shared between two or even three different
   litigants (and their advisers) pursuing different
   entities where the issues were the same. Also, it
   may be useful to be able to spread at least some
   of the costs of expert witnesses between the
   different cases.

6. *Loan from lawyer.* This is a difficult area: do the
   Bar Rules (or local equivalent) allow this? In
   practice, all over the world some lawyers may
   occasionally help somebody in distress (if they
   can) and take the view that, if the litigant does
   not win, they too will lose but both parties
   will win if the litigant wins their case. Not all
   lawyers do this, and some frown on the practice.
   Moreover, not all specialised lawyers can afford
   to do this. Some specialised firms in the United
   States do divorce work purely on this basis but
   only take on small numbers of carefully chosen
   litigants; however, many firms will give credit

in divorce cases where they are pretty sure that they will succeed in gaining an enforceable judgment.

7. *Contingency fee agreements (CFAs).* Broadly speaking, in some countries some lawyers can work on the basis that they uplift their fees if they win (ordinarily either an enhancement to the usual hourly rates or a share of the award). There are many variations and it is country-dependent. A firm that is willing to take a risk may be indicating faith in the case. All firms taking a risk on this basis want to gain more at the end of the case than they are risking.

8. *Litigation funders.*

   – There has been a revolution in this area, at least in Anglo-Saxon countries/the USA. There are now many litigation funders with a multitude of different approaches. Ordinarily they like the law firm involved to have some skin in the game so this approach would be difficult in countries that do not allow CFAs.

   – Litigation funders expect to be paid a multiple of their investment. They may invest a fixed amount or offer continuing investment with some form of 'ratchet' (terms can vary).

- Funders are going to take a big slice of the
  eventual award, there is no two ways about
  that, and they only support some cases. They
  want to know that they are almost certain
  to win, that any opinion offered by counsel
  and/or the lawyers in the case is favourable,
  that the claim makes sense and the amount
  claimed stacks up. Even then, in broad terms
  they are likely to want at least three times
  their investment back.

- There are many litigation funders, so many
  deals are possible. There are specialist
  publications dealing solely with this field,
  containing comparison tables for different
  funders. Ordinarily litigation funding does
  not work for smaller claims, and it will not
  work for difficult cases, but it is often an
  option and should be explored with your
  legal team at the beginning.

- One advantage of having a funder on board is
  that it tends to intimidate the opposition, who
  now know you are not likely to run out of
  money. The disadvantages are a much lower
  award at the end and the funder may want
  some control over the litigation.

9. *After-the-event insurance (ATE).* It is possible to buy insurance against the risk of an adverse costs order. Premiums can be large, and this is probably best suited for bigger claims where costs are (relatively) a smaller percentage of the overall claim.

10. *Other insurance.* Most professional firms carry professional indemnity insurance and a lot of financial institutions carry directors and officers (D&O) cover, which can be useful. Private litigants sometimes overlook the existence of the litigation cover tacked onto household policies. One of the biggest suppliers of the latter type of cover insists that litigants use lawyers from its own list, which might suit your claim but might tie you to a firm with little experience in your area.

CONCLUSIONS

- Proceed with caution – litigation is expensive.
- If you cannot finish the journey, do not start it.
- Think through the constraints on you before you start.

- Examine carefully all the options at the beginning.

- Discuss the equations involved with your advisers at the outset.

7
Expert Evidence: Lies & Damned Lies

Before looking at how and why evidence goes wrong, what you can do about it, what expert witnesses are, when they should be used and how they can help, it is instructive to first look at what evidence is.

What is evidence?

A witness is by definition someone who saw, heard or did something relevant to the matter in issue; ordinarily, a person who witnesses something, saw, heard or smelt it happen. Unfortunately, as soon as you google the word witness, an important and worrying distortion begins, with all sorts of definitions linked to the legal world.

An expert witness is almost a contradiction in terms. Time after time, on behalf of litigants, I have objected to evidence and so-called witnesses, because they knew little or nothing of the events in question, and their written or verbal statements were devoid of factual content, containing arguments and 'averrals' drafted by lawyers. The rules of evidence properly applied should knock this sort of thing on the head; indeed, judges can sometimes be quite acerbic and correctly so.

A witness statement should be written from the 'I' perspective and give a first-hand account of what has been done, heard, smelt or seen. Anything moving away from that formula is at the start of a very slippery slope. If the person in question 'was not there' or 'did not do it', why is their statement being admitted at all? Courts in the Commonwealth and elsewhere often lose sight of basics and enormous injustices follow. Family courts are notorious for relaxing and bending the rules with devastating results. Judges fudge the issue by saying that such evidence has less weight, a nebulous, unpoliceable concept, giving *carte blanche* to the unscrupulous simply to make up what they need, or to gild the lily.[21]

As have other practitioners, I have noted that, all too often, the modern penchant, so incredibly helpful in many respects, for mediating cases to a close and disposing of disputes without trials, exacerbates matters, as fewer and fewer witnesses are ever questioned about the evidence they have given. The remedy, having a trial and cross-examining witnesses, is expensive and can give rise to uncertain results. I deal with some examples below.

One of the worst examples I saw was in a family case, where a nanny's email, written for her by the mother's lawyers, was admitted as evidence. It was a commentary designed to assist one side. The young lady was 'nervous' so she was excused from giving evidence, even though the litigant applied for her so to do; but a neatly pejorative, wholly untestable document, written by the other side's lawyer, became 'evidence'.

---

21   CSAFE, 'Misuse of statistics in the court room: The Sally Clark case', 18 February 2018https://forensicstats.org/blog/2018/02/16/misuse -statistics-courtroom-sally-clark-case); this case shows how miscalculated probabilities resulted in a miscarriage of justice.

Right-thinking litigants, and their lawyers, need to hold the judge's feet to the fire, or justice has no chance of being done. False, 'helpful', lawyer-drafted evidence is a serious epidemic and an all-pervasive rot, adversely affecting the fabric of society and of justice.

A famous case in England involved a well-known and much-liked businessman. People came forward in droves to give 'helpful' support and testimony on his behalf, so the opposition took the point and tested the evidence. The judge found against the businessman, then referred the papers to the Director of Public Prosecutions, who brought prosecutions: over a dozen people were convicted and many jailed for giving false testimony. These were people of previously good character, who had become caught up in the moment.

This is not a commentary on human nature and the psychology of the herd. The only advice I can really give is, 'If you are in the right, stick to your guns', and please remember that there are websites giving a direct route to suppliers who will write a student's essay, produce a false invoice or draft a legal document for a few pounds.

A document is only evidence of its own content (it says what it says): the content is not true just because it has been written down, and if a document says who wrote it, when or where, these details need to be checked. Evidence is not proof.

The problem does not rest with private litigants or defendants. In criminal trials, all too often the prosecution are at it as well. Out-and-out false evidence by policemen is a common occurrence and has been for decades, as is gilding the lily.[22]

Before going on to give further examples, the best advice I can give (and repeat) is to be aware of the realities of human nature and, if need be, to stand your ground, be pedantic – a competent lawyer looking at a witness statement can often spot numerous tell-tales and pointers within the document.

There are relaxations for 'interlocutory' hearings (hearings that are not final), to allow evidence to be put forward by advisers and by company officers and the like. Such evidence can relate, not just to the person giving it, but to others and the basis for that is, in realistic terms, quite sound, because it enables the case to move

---

22 Brown, D. 'Accused Hillsborough trio altered witness statements to cover up police failings', *The Times*, 21 April 2021, www.thetimes.co .uk/article/hillsborough-accused-altered-witness-statements-to-cover -up-police-failings-j8sp7l8ww

on. Often the evidence is not at issue; but sometimes it is, and it is therefore capable of abuse.

An interlocutory 'affidavit' should contain an affirmation along these lines:

'I, Mr White of Black Forest Farm, make oath and swear as follows:

That the contents of this Affidavit, where known to me, are true and where not known to me are true to the best of my knowledge, information and belief (*based on the following sources which I identify below*).'

So far so good, but not only is this obviously open to abuse, but most affidavits of this nature either do not have the words in brackets or simply fail to identify any sources for the 'evidence' they contain. Such affidavits should be challenged as a matter of course. I and others have done this to great effect but all too often the judge grunts 'that goes to weight' and moves on.[23] In theory, at an interlocutory hearing cross-examining on the

---

23 Judges are supposed to decide which evidence can and should be relied on, not to say "perhaps" or "sort of" which is the implication of this phrase.

content of an affidavit should be permitted, unfortunately in practice too many judges cannot be bothered.

This is a truly grim topic, lightened and darkened by some examples.

HOT AIR

I was sitting behind a young Jamaican barrister in a West Indies court. The opposition had imported a leading London silk (QC), relying on an affidavit from a solicitor in a 'magic circle' or elite UK firm. Having let the QC run on for a while, our barrister pointed out to the presiding judge that the affidavit:

1. had been sworn by somebody who had no first-hand knowledge of the case, and

2. consisted almost entirely of submissions and legal argument.

The judge asked for an explanation. 'Madam, we do this all the time, in Chancery Division,' oiled the QC disingenuously.

'Really?' replied Her Ladyship. 'Well, you might do that in your Chancery Division, but you are not doing it in my court'. The affidavit was not admitted into evidence.

Many judges, in many countries, are happy to do the needful. I might wish that more did so, but then I am representing one side. The law is clear, but its implementation can vary and sometimes it is implemented badly or not at all.

Returning to interlocutory affidavits, evidence for the trial must say 'The content of my witness statement/ affidavit *is known to me and is true'*. Anything else should be treated with great suspicion.

On the grim topic of manufacturing evidence, I have a little inside knowledge of the Hillsborough disaster, from a shocked and honest policeman who was working at the ground that day. The South Yorkshire police went into overdrive after the event to manufacture witness evidence from policemen. That it happened was bad, but not shocking; that it was organised at a high level and implemented throughout the ranks as a matter of policy, was and is shocking.[24]

As a junior defence barrister I had a stock of questions for police witnesses, starting with 'Are the pages in

---

24 Conn, D., 'Hillsborough disaster: deadly mistakes and lies that lasted decades', *The Guardian*, 26 April 2016, www.theguardian.com/football /2016/apr/26/hillsborough-disaster-deadly-mistakes-and-lies-that -lasted-decades.

your notebook numbered?', through 'If not, why not?', 'Why are so many pages missing?', 'Do you not use your notebook chronologically?', to 'Why is Sunday coming after Wednesday?' and several others.

Given an alert judge, the consequences of such questioning were intermittently devastating for the prosecution. The other thing to do after police officers had read their evidence from their notebook was to say, 'Officer, please pass me your notebook so I can read what it says'. Sometimes I was allowed to, and at other times it was like a form of heresy: disallowed by the judge for reasons I can only guess at.

INTERVIEW UNDER COMPULSION

In a recent case, HMRC required a police officer to be interviewed 'under compulsion'. Interviews under compulsion are rare, and used only for the most serious crimes. The power to compel witness testimony is one which should be used exceedingly sparingly and in the rarest of circumstances by the prosecution.

Anyway, the compelled questioning went as follows:

HMRC: Officer, do you agree that...

Police officer: Eh?

HMRC: For transparency, I should say that I have a witness statement from Mr O…now, do you agree?

Not only had Mr O never given a witness statement, but when a draft witness statement had been given to him to sign, it was so manifestly false that not only did he say so and refuse to sign it, but he unceremoniously and summarily evicted the officers from his premises.

The charges were dropped.

OVER-PREPARATION

When cross-examining a witness for insurance underwriters, the questioning went as follows:

PS: Is the evidence you have given from memory?

Witness: Yes.

PS: Do you remember what happened?

W: Yes.

PS: Are you sure?

W: Yes.

PS: How good is your memory?

W: Very good.

PS: Please show the court your right hand and read what is written on it.

W: 'Things to tell the court'...

Expert evidence

If a witness is someone who saw, heard, did or smelt, what is an expert witness? A contradiction in terms? Surely you cannot become a witness in the true sense by design, let alone after the event, so what are they and what do they do?

The rationale for their existence is to provide expertise, knowledge and experience in relation to areas beyond the knowledge and abilities of ordinary folk (and judges). Expert witnesses are informers, not arbiters. They are there, in theory at least, to assist the decision-making process, to help the judge or tribunal understand the facts. Uniquely, experts are allowed to express opinions; witnesses of fact are supposed to tell the court *only* what they saw, heard, did, smelt and should never be encouraged to speculate.

Good uses of expert evidence are in relation to scientific matters, industry usages, eg specialist financial instruments, and of course, in relation to forensic medicine. They can and do inform courts what things mean, how things work, how an industry works, what normally happens and the consequences of certain actions in relation to a given set of circumstances.

An easy example, and there are many, would be: did this bullet come from this gun? If so, why do you say that?

Expert witnesses are an enormous help to courts in many scenarios; but while a lot goes right, a lot also goes wrong. Experts are theoretically, and sometimes in practice, independent of the side that calls them. This is a standard attestation used by expert witnesses:

I have been instructed by [Name].

I understand that my paramount duty is to provide impartial expert assistance to the Court. This report has not been prepared with the objective of supporting [Name]. In this respect, I declare that:

1. I understand that my duty in providing written reports and giving evidence is to help the court and that this duty overrides any

obligation to the parties that engaged me. I confirm that I have complied with and will continue to comply with this duty;

2. I confirm that, insofar as the facts stated in this report are within my knowledge, I have made clear which facts they are and I believe them to be true and that the opinions I have expressed herein represent my true and complete professional opinion;

3. I have endeavoured to include in my report those matters which I have knowledge of or of which I have been made aware that might adversely affect the validity of my opinion;

4. I have indicated the sources of all information I have used;

5. I have not, without forming an independent view, included or excluded anything which has been suggested to me by others, in particular, my instructing lawyers and/or the directors;

6. I will notify those instructing me immediately and confirm in writing if for any reason my existing report requires any correction or qualification;

7. I understand that:

   (a) My report, subject to any corrections before swearing as to its correctness, will form the evidence to given under oath or affirmation;

   (b) I may be cross-examined on my report by a cross-examiner assisted by an expert;

   (c) I am likely to be the subject of public adverse criticism by the judge if the court concludes that I have not taken reasonable care in trying to meet the standards set out above;

8. I confirm that I have not entered into any arrangement where the amount or payment of my fees is in any way dependent on the outcome of the case(s).

I, [expert witness's name], accept no responsibility to any other party for breaches of the above confidentiality clauses, or for any opinions expressed or information included in this report and shall not be liable for any loss, damage or expense whatsoever nature which is caused by their reliance on my report.

This report must not be construed as
expressing opinions on matters of law, which
are for the Court to determine.

You will note that their evidence stands alone; they
expect to be criticised if they give inadequate or misleading evidence; they owe duties directly to the court
and not to the party paying them to testify. So far so
good.

Unfortunately, a common and almost universal trend
in litigation is to have an expert witness on each side,
each reaching a different conclusion to the other. In
other words, each litigant will find and field an expert
who agrees with its views. At this stage, some experts
may well have stopped helping the court and be moving away from purity and real judicial assistance into
argument, opinion and litigant aid.

How do you find a suitable, ie competent and compelling, expert? Firstly, tell the truth. If you have a
good case and you are in the right (and most people
know when they are) when you start reaching out
this will come across. Secondly, there are many ways
of reaching out: for example, there are associations
of professional witnesses. Thirdly, start not only by

looking at their professional qualifications, which you may not understand, but by trying to get a feel for the expert as a person. Can you work with them? Are they convincing? Are they convinced? If push comes to shove their personal presence and demeanour may be factors that persuade a judge to give their evidence 'weight'. In evaluating potential witnesses the human touch is important.

Good expert witnesses

Experts who are competent, independent adults can save the parties and everybody else involved a lot of time and money. They will ordinarily be directed to meet their opposite number at a fairly early stage to see what they can agree on and then what they disagree on. You can then get from them a set of agreed facts and a series of issues on which they do not agree or take slightly different views.

Examples that I have seen of this going right have been in Switzerland. In a case which involved points of Swiss law, the two experts, independently, came up with almost exactly the same position, save that the other side's expert was slightly more strongly in my favour than my own. Now that is real expert evidence and that is real justice and real law coming out. I wish I had seen more of this in my career.

How do you undermine and attack an expert witness?

There are obvious hygiene checks to be undertaken if you do not believe the opposite number's expert witness or what they are saying. These hygiene checks ought also to be undertaken before you employ your own expert witness, to investigate their qualifications. This can be done on a relatively low-key, open source basis.

Several cases have been reported of experts who turn out to have no university degree, or one from a doubtful university[25]. Bogus qualifications exist. What do the 'expert's' qualifications mean, who are they, where do they work? There are due diligence questions in relation to any witnesses that you are going to employ, let alone any that are employed against you.

To instil rigour you need knowledge or an understanding of the subject matter. Once you acquire that,

---

25 Coleman, C., 'Carbon credit fraud trial collapses as expert witness was no expert', *BBC News*, 30 May 2019, www.bbc.co.uk/news/uk-48444605.

and you can be helped to do this by your own expert or by your own research, analysing evidence nearly always boils down to basic logic and basic probabilities, gaining a careful understanding of facts and concepts. An impugned or undermined expert may or may not stick to their guns under cross-examination, but your position should be logical. The presence of logic and reasoning should be what gets the judge on your side, and their absence should undermine the opposition. Sometimes judges understand the reasoning, sometimes they do not and sometimes they duck the question by simply preferring one expert's delivery to another's. A judge may be driven by mistaken impressions, just like anybody else. I have seen it happen more often than I am comfortable with.

Before going on let us look at some other examples of evidence going wrong. All humans are fallible, all humans have a dark side. Human beings who are feted and respected as experts and whose opinions hold sway sometimes get carried away with themselves. They become the ultimate arbiters. In England there was a shocking example where a number of perfectly innocent parents were given long prison sentences for 'child abuse', all on the say so of two doctors applying a technique they did not understand, which was later discredited.[26] The horror that those parents went through is unimaginable. They were convicted of harming their nearest and dearest, had their children taken away from them, they lost their reputations, livelihoods and assets and some committed suicide.

MORE HORROR

Some years ago, a young lady in desperate circumstances (Miss Q), placed under what was, in effect, house arrest, with no assets and few advisers, became involved in a custody suit. She said she had been a single parent for about seven years, because her husband, the father of their children, was not that interested and led an erratic lifestyle. When he wanted to come back into her life, she said no; she had a boyfriend by that stage. Her husband manufactured a raft of allegations that, largely speaking, should have been easy to disprove.

Men and women in relationships can take rejection very badly. This can cause them to act in ways that could best be described as 'wicked'. Common sense, logic, human givens and human basics can escape professionals brought in to assess what they say.

---

26 Pain, A., '20 years on from the Cleveland Child Sex Abuse Scandal', *GazetteLive*, 8 July 2008, www.gazettelive.co.uk/news/local-news/20 -years-cleveland-child-sex-3729871.

The Children and Family Court Advisory and Support Service (CAFCASS) are treated like officers of the court and are largely beyond reproach. That was little help to this young, highly distressed lady. Her advisers told her to agree to a psychological assessment proposed by a counsellor approved by CAFCASS, who for some reason had taken to the husband.

Somehow Miss Q became aware that the CAFCASS counsellor was spending time with the 'family psychologist', who should have been carrying out the assessment independently (though no records or notes of their meetings were kept).

When questioning an expert, the first question is, 'What facts did you establish, and what assumptions of fact have you made?' Examining the psychologist's report was very instructive.

A primary function of experts is to make their expertise and knowledge capable of assimilation by ordinary people: this report failed completely to do that. Pages and pages of it were utterly unintelligible, not only to Miss Q but to her educated advisers, of which I had become one on a *pro bono* basis. It was written like a poor-quality legal opinion, with numerous citations, professional jargon and reliance upon the work and authorities of others. Looked at objectively, it failed the basic smell test.

Miss Q, in her mid-thirties, had not been asked about any aspect of her life since she had turned seventeen.

The author also quoted a professional body to which she belonged and which is recognised in England, so we looked up what that body said about how to conduct interviews and assessments of this kind, and the author had failed on every point.

We examined the authorities cited in the report and found that they did not support the interpretation put on them. The authorities in question had been heavily qualified, eg had stated that a particular interpretation only applies in stated circumstances; but the psychologist had made no reference to those circumstances.

We helped Miss Q win. She was released from house arrest and went home with her children. It could, however, have all gone horribly wrong.

Judicial systems are poor at admitting mistakes, let alone saying sorry or providing any form of monetary or other compensation. For example, although a judge ordered Miss Q be freed, he refused to produce a judgment, perhaps because a judgment would have had to say all is not well with the system. Many wrongly convicted prisoners have been released from jails as a result of the introduction of DNA evidence: all of a sudden it was found that they were telling the truth. The conditions for launching an appeal and the restrictions on compensation are shocking. Some forensic experts are little more than evidence factories, secure in the knowledge that nobody has the time, the resource or the expertise to challenge them.

CONCLUSION

- Trust nothing and nobody unless there is good reason so to do.

- If something is not right, stand your ground.

- Make sure you have access, where possible, to the raw material upon which any evidence is based.

- Take no prisoners – false testimony is a scourge upon society.

8
Institutions And Mis-selling

Institutions are very good at mis-selling, which means there are two topics here. Let us start with what they do and then look at what you can do to gain restitution.

A common misconception remains widespread, especially among those who remember old-fashioned high streets, that institutions and businesses of any size are run by the great and the good, that they are almost by definition reputable and can be trusted to advise in the same way as every other professional.

The first thing to realise is that this is not so; the second is to realise that as defendants they are obdurate, well-heeled and shameless. Banks alone have been fined billions in recent years, for activities including money laundering, rigging LIBOR (the reference rate used to set virtually all loan rates), aiding tax fraud, breaking government sanctions on several unpleasant countries and misleading investors. I am not convinced that the fines for these breaches have made a whit of difference. More and more individuals employed by banks are now being taken to court, but they represent a small part of the 'sharp end'. Again, I do not think the deterrent is effective. Deterrence comes from certainty of detection and sanctions that reflect the harm done.

The Conduct Cost Projects (CCP) Research Foundation reports that between 2012 and 2016 the world's top twenty banks were made to pay fines for misconduct amounting to £264 billion. In other words almost all twenty were at it. These 'misconducts' involved huge sums of money: these were not minor infractions without consequences. In 2014 alone the Bank of America incurred £22.12 billion in fines of which £12.65 billion was a settlement with the US Department of Trade for fraud.

Do not trust people or institutions who have been found guilty of fraud: fraud is dishonesty and that's that.

Between 2012 and 2016 fines for mis-selling mortgages, primarily to individuals, totalled £65.84 billion; in 2018 Royal Bank of Scotland (RBS) International was fined $4.9 billion by the US Department of Justice for mis-selling offences.[27]. These were ordinary people lacking the expertise necessary to protect themselves. They have even less chance of redress after the event.

What does this tell us? The answer, in the vernacular, is that ripping off customers has been found to be a day-to-day activity for many financial institutions by regulators and courts in many countries (including the UK).

PAYMENT PROTECTION INSURANCE (PPI)

The PPI scandal went on for nearly two decades. Banks knowingly scammed their customers, little deterred by the regulator. PPI was supposed to be a cushion if the customer lost their job; the idea was that the customer's loan repayments would be covered if they lost their job or became ill.

---

27 Kollewe, J., 'RBS settles US Department of Justice investigation with $4.9bn fine', *The Guardian*, 10 May 2018, www.theguardian .com/business/2018/may/10/rbs-settles-us-department-of-justice -investigation-with-49bn-fine.

The following facts were well known to those who sold this insurance:

1. *Expensive* – premiums often 20% of loan repayments and sometimes over 50%; *and*

2. *Ineffective* – small print limited the illnesses and other conditions that were covered; *and*

3. *Mis-sold* – often, the customer did not know it was included in the 'package' they bought; or were told no PPI, no loan; *and*

4. *Dishonestly sold* – to people such as the self-employed who were not actually covered by the insurance; *and*

5. *Inefficient* – claimants faced delays manufactured by a complicated claims procedure.

The whole thing was dishonest from top to bottom, and the people selling it knew, for example, that self-employed people do not have a salary, so would not be able to claim.

The Financial Services Authority (as it then was; FSA) started to fine banks for mis-selling PPI in 2006. In 2008 the Alliance and Leicester was fined £7 million, when the FSA ruled that its staff were being trained to 'put pressure on customers who questioned inclusion of PPI in their quotation'. By 2007 the Office of Fair Trading was involved and in mid-2008 it was reported that one in three loan customers had been sold worthless insurance. It had long been known that some people had been mis-sold PPI, but most people were amazed to discover the scale of the dishonesty. It appears that salespeople were chasing commissions and their bosses were chasing profits – where was the sense of responsibility to the customer, let alone ordinary human decency?

Responsibility to customers does not seem to have occurred to the banks that sold PPI; a series of cases have shown that the front line were heavily incentivised to do so and the boardroom looked purely at profit, and saw themselves as protected from any meaningful deterrent.

Swaps

Starting about 2012, my firm were involved in a number of cases linked to the rigging of LIBOR and the mis-selling of swaps. We started knowing little about the matter, commissioned our own in-house intelligence report and completed our front-end load.

This is a chapter about institutions and mis-selling, so I am not going to comment much on a particular product, because we are looking here at the broader picture. However, it might be helpful to use these as a case study.

When presented with a novel problem what did we do?

1. We spoke to colleagues in this field in other jurisdictions so we could cross-fertilise knowledge and expertise.

2. We methodically went through every piece of open source intelligence we could find.

3. We found whistleblowers, people who had previously been on the inside who could be persuaded to brief us on the issues involved.

4. We found technical experts who could draw the comparison between what was sold and what should have been sold.

5. We studied to the code of practice for lenders operating in those areas, and found it was not being enforced.

What did we discover?

Banks work in a pyramid structure: bank managers are effectively the organisation's interface with customers, ie the shop front. All bank managers are given annual targets in writing, which are adjusted each year. Targets depend on a number of factors including the previous year's performance and the nature of the catchment area, ie the number and disposition of targets within the area within which the branch is allowed to look for customers.

When targets are met or exceeded significant bonuses are paid, often a high percentage of basic salary. For some bank staff, total pay contains more bonus than salary. Failure to meet targets is almost universally seen as a bar to promotion or a trigger for redundancy.

Historically, a bank manager had done his job if (s)he lent money to his/her clients, and borrowed it back from them (by selling them accounts): that was how banks worked. Over the years bank managers have been given more and more other 'products' to sell: mortgages, insurance, pensions, interest rate fixes and several more sophisticated instruments. The more profitable products were assigned to a higher 'tier' and the bank manager was told how many to sell in each tier. Remember, profit for the bank comes out of the customer's money.

Most financial institutions, including banks, have departments that develop products to be sold to the public and increase profits for the selling institution. Where the seller is the counter-party[28] to the contract involved, their financial interest is different from yours and might even be diametrically opposed to yours; it is a bit like allowing a bookmaker to sell bets, not just take them.

One former salesperson described matters as follows:

'On a weekly basis a rocket scientist came to a sales meeting attended by some fifty sales staff with new products to sell to the bank's client base. Most of us did not understand what the product was or how it worked, let alone its implications. We were given leads by our employer in relation to existing account holders; there was never any question of the customers asking for the product, we were product-led.'[29]

---

28 The party on the other side of the contract who gains or loses directly according to how well or badly the customer does.
29 This an extract from a witness statement for a trial in which I dealt.

Financial institutions put in place specialist sales teams, recruited, trained, paid by commissions and other incentives to sell products to benefit the bank, insurance company, stockbroker...Some banks describe them to the outside world as corporate advisers. They are not there to advise, they are there to sell.

Typical practice is for a salesperson to be assigned a geographical area, then introduced to bank managers in that area. Without the bank manager's knowledge of the customer and their finances the sales teams would be severely hampered; armed with that knowledge and with opportunities to issue ultimatums, ie 'take this product or we will not give you a loan', selling is like shooting fish in a barrel. It was put this way by Tim Kerr, QC, in *Crestsign Ltd v National Westminster Bank plc* [2014] EWHC 3095 (Ch):

> 'For the banks, I heard oral evidence from Mr S[...] F[...], a relationship manager employed by NatWest, from Mr N[...] G[...], who at the material time was employed by RBS [Royal Bank of Scotland] as an interest rate risk manager responsible for introducing the bank's derivative products to customers, and arranging interest rate management [IRM] transactions.

Mr G[...] is a salesman to his bones as well
as, then and now, an expert on IRM products.
His performance at the meeting was, I am
satisfied, polished, as it was when he gave
evidence before me.'

The sales teams are not there to advise anybody on the
suitability of the products, they are there to sell them,
whatever they may imply at the time of sale. Once the
deal is done, banks then issue documentation designed
to exclude all liability for 'advice' given.

From the same case (emphasis mine):

'In sum, the banks did not provide misleading
information. They did provide negligent
advice *but they successfully excluded any duty not
to do so*. They did not show themselves worthy
of the trust [the litigant] placed in them, but
unfortunately for Crestsign, the common law
provides it with no remedy because the banks
successfully disclaimed responsibility for the
advice they gave on the suitability of the swap
which was negligent but not actionable.'

As an aside Mr Kerr was never provided with the full
picture in relation to the activities of the banks relative
to the fixing of LIBOR.

As set out above, the salespeople are armed with a sales planner, a target for the year and a list of 'prospects' from bank managers. The sales planner provides a running update on commission generated and the amount of time and therefore money spent per lead. The cost of individual meetings is calculated backwards from the overall target and in some cases the banks impose a threshold of no less than £5,000 to be generated per meeting. Some sales planners are updated daily and sent electronically back to the salesperson's supervisor.

Interest rate hedging products, in particular, have been hugely profitable for banks. These are a one-way bet. In the cases my firm handled, purchasers could not get out of these products without paying huge exit charges, the size and nature of which had not been communicated to them before sale, and had signed documentation which was highly disadvantageous to them in a legal context. Many good and successful businesses went bankrupt.

What has happened is that the culture within banks has collapsed. You can now buy many books on the subject and read a lot of articles about it. Old-fashioned bank managers are long gone. Banks played a significant part in the 2008 recession and may well be a significant factor in the next one.

The fact that this sort of behaviour has become endemic was brought home very clearly to me when one of our support staff came to me after typing a report to a litigant (on this very subject) to say that she had recently had a bequest; her mum had left her some money in her will. Within hours of what (for this lady) was an abnormally large amount of money being paid into her bank account people from her bank were phoning her up to try to sell her their products. What happened to her confidentiality?

Common themes in mis-selling

Bear in mind how salespeople are incentivised and the pyramid structure of most financial services companies (especially banks). In the cases our firm handled, customers had not been informed:

1. Even in outline, what the product really was, and sometimes thoroughly misled as to what it was; one of our clients, who had an interest rate swap, thought it was some type of life insurance;

2. That their trade confirmations or purchase notes would exclude liability for misrepresentation, ie rights were taken away after the sale;

3. When better protection or products could be obtained from the same institution for lower prices;

4. That unwinding these transactions would be so expensive as to make it impossible;

5. Conversely, of terms allowing the banks to step out of the transaction as and when they felt like it with few, if any, penalties;

6. That the seller stood to benefit if the customer lost money on swaps; and

7. that the sellers sold swaps on to other institutions, so the customer did not have an enduring relationship with the institution that sold them the swap.

Conversely, customers were told that flexibility and renegotiation were allowed for, although the documentation they signed meant exactly the opposite.

In short, what we discovered was that clients were being taken advantage of by the very people that they trusted. That it was an endemic, systemised exploitation of knowledge and relationships.

Now having looked in bald terms at the nature of the problem, if you are faced with similar exploitation what can you do about it?

Beating Goliath

My firm has won all of the cases I describe in this chapter. It was not easy, but:

- In our last three major cases the three litigants were awarded £45 million, for a total cost of £1.5 million split between them.

- A high street litigant was awarded over £280,000 for a £3,000 spend (ie our fees).

It is possible, but it is not easy. How do you do it?

The usual principles apply but you have a shameless adversary, often disingenuous and possessed of virtually unlimited resources. Those are the obstacles. On the positive side you may find:

1. *Fellow litigants.* Institutions do not normally just defraud one person; there may well be a lot of others. They all have knowledge and insights

and there is strength in numbers for victims, in terms both of finance and of knowledge.

2. *Causes célèbres.* Attract multiple investigations and commentaries. There are still some good journalists out there so you can end up with a mine of open source materials.

3. *Whistleblowers.* People employed in unethical organisations sometimes do not like it and then for moral or personal reasons go public. Some that may not want their names attributed may still be happy to provide information.

4. *Publicity.* Mucky institutions really dislike publicity; creatures living under stones do not like spotlights. It is a perfectly permissible and indeed often sensible strategy to brief journalists. Litigants can do it direct: journalists can be very helpful (but have their own agenda). Two defendants were brave and hostile until we actually served proceedings, at which stage they worried about the adverse publicity and did a deal.

5. The same thing goes for *Members of Parliament* or if dealing outside the United Kingdom, regional and national legislators.

6. *Regulators.* While no case I have prosecuted in Jersey received any help from the regulator, other countries have regulators who take action, sometimes perfunctory, sometimes helpful.

7. *Pressure groups, support groups and fellow victims.* Moral support is in itself a powerful aid, as is the opportunity to exchange information and resources..

8. *Enforcement.* If you win, enforcing a judgment is normally not a problem, unless the institution goes bust: HBOS, Northern Rock and others went under.

There is one further major point. In most countries, as part of the litigation process litigants have to produce all relevant documents. If you are suing an institution, do not hold your breath, pursue them tenaciously and be prepared to be told less than the whole story. Following the money is a good rule. How did they collate and deploy the information they disclose about how much money they made and who got it? Push the right buttons during discovery and sometimes the attitude of the other side changes overnight, as liability for the malfeasance might be pushed further up, nearer to the real decisionmakers. If you can pressure the real decisionmakers, ie not the people in the front line who get hung out to dry, you are more likely to obtain a settlement.

Sinel's now know a lot about how banks collate and distribute information in relation to mis-sold products. It is extremely important knowledge. We also now know a lot about their internal systems.

I have not said much about the law. The legal matrix follows from the factual matrix. Different countries have different systems of law. Banks are adept at producing 'boilerplate' documentation, so if you can prove fraud, it solves a lot of problems: as I explained in Chapter 5, 'fraud unravels all'.

This example illustrates the points above.

CANTRADE

One of my earlier successes was acting for a fund manager against Cantrade Bank, a subsidiary of UBS. To cut a long story short, the bank maintained a currency trader was unrelated to it, though he lived in a house that the bank owned. Each forex trade attracted a four percentage-in-points (PIP) charge by the bank, which was then split equally between the bank and the trader. This was an incentive to 'churn'.[30] The litigant unwittingly employed a crooked accountant (who later served time) who issued false valuations, while its bank balances were difficult to follow – these were trading accounts with multiple transactions over them.

The case became a *cause célèbre* because the bank were utterly unrepentant and the investors became crosser and more vocal. A relatively small (£20 million) fraud became global news, attracting coverage in the *Wall Street Journal*, *Financial Times* and elsewhere.[31]

Aggravating factors included conflict of interest on the committee running banking regulations, Cantrade complaining to the Law Society about me and the chairman of the regulatory committee suing me for defamation, all of which we beat off after appealing over the head of Jersey's Attorney-General to the Home Office. In due course the bank was fined £2 million, the trader got four years and the accountant who had been certifying his figures got two and a half years.

Cantrade appealed and the case ploughed on; after a RICO action in the United States they came to the table. At this stage Cantrade had brought

---

30 'Churning' means generating unnecessary trades to drive up commission or fees.
31 Sesit, M.R., 'USB subsidiary in Jersey is charged with fraud', *Wall Street Journal*, 29 October 1996, www.wsj.com/articles/SB846539634616514500.

in a huge firm from England which produced a settlement agreement. As we puzzled over it we noticed there was no confidentiality clause. We thought, not unnaturally, that Cantrade planned to settle the action, claim this was in the interests of the investors, then throw mud at the fund managers, who had financed the recovery action on behalf of the investors.

The settlement document was signed late one evening in Switzerland, and we went to the press to deflect the anticipated adverse PR campaign. It was duly all over the newspapers the next day. We then heard directly from Cantrade who asked us, 'What about the confidentiality clause?' We suggested they speak to their lawyers. I would very much have liked to have been a fly on the wall for that meeting.

My firm's website (https://sintelglobal.co.uk) offers material, including a sample intelligence report that my firm produced, which may be helpful if you are thinking of suing a bank or other financial institution (www.sintelglobal.co.uk/build/img/New_PDF_Sinel _Blog.pdf).

9

Divorces And High-Net-Worth Divorces (HNW)

The aim in divorce proceedings is to get a fair settlement with the minimum disruption, expense of time and money and the least possible emotional damage to those involved (who may not be limited to the couple).

You may say the same applies for any case but there are different aspects to divorce. How it ends depends on the attitude of the couple and their advisers. There are varying shades of complexity and hostility. It is common to encounter non-disclosing spouses, overly ambitious and badly advised spouses and spouses who want to deal amicably; people come in all shades.

This chapter deals mainly with spouses who will not disclose what the court requires them to.

We mentioned FDRs in Chapter 4. Financial Dispute Resolutions, a form of directed mediation, are exceptionally helpful in complex, high-value cases. However, they only work once both parties' assets have been fully ascertained.

What is a HNW divorce?

HNW divorces have common features:

1. Significant wealth which has been either made or inherited

2. One party creating or controlling more of the wealth or inheritance than the other

3. Spouses making varying types of contribution, from homemaker to genuine business partner

4. Assets in different countries, nearly always with an offshore element and a degree of structuring; what that means in practice is trusts, companies, foundations and a number of cross-border considerations

5. In a small percentage of cases husband and wife having a business, producing very significant wealth, which has taken off owing to the equal efforts of both spouses

In a divorce of this nature, it is important to pick the right advisers at the beginning. Things can go wrong when a strictly matrimonial practitioner has been picked to act for one of the parties. Divorces of this nature can need a blend of skills which include: a. an intelligence gathering arm, in-house or external; b. accountancy support and c. regrettably sometimes, litigation skills more often found in commercial practice, covering injunctions, search orders and third-party disclosure orders.

It is difficult to rectify a position which has already deteriorated. Given latitude an unscrupulous spouse who has decided to hide their assets or circumvent the judicial process in some fashion could have made considerable progress. Putting the genie back in the bottle can be a struggle.

Each case depends on its own facts but identifying and recovering assets concealed by defaulting spouses could be a book in itself, so I will only partially address it here.

The other point to make at this juncture is that the points made in this chapter are not limited to any one jurisdiction but should apply in many jurisdictions.

Some disputes between genuinely equal business partners can have tragic outcomes, sometimes best resolved (if possible) by the use of appropriate Alternative Dispute Resolution skills (FDRs in particular), because a fight involving the goose that laid the golden egg can end up killing the goose.

In the event that you suspect that your spouse is not going to play by the rules, then before asking questions formally or informally build up a picture of assets, key personnel, companies and related. There are a number of ways to do this. Human intelligence is of course very important:

1. Even when little involved in their partner's business, spouses tend to know a lot more than they think, which can often provide investigators and lawyers with valuable leads.

2. lot of legitimate sources of information can be mined before getting under way: disaffected business partners, family members, mistresses, former lovers and employees can be useful

sources of intelligence, without having to dig especially deeply.

3. Publicly available information, open source documentation and the like, if trawled carefully, can yield dividends.

Two case studies discuss the legitimate use of open source and human intelligence:

TWO HOUSEHOLDS

We discovered that a defaulting spouse had another house and another child. Leaving on one side the devastating impact of this information on the litigant, the fact that there was another wholly unencumbered asset available for distribution, which could not have been found without a degree of investigation, was very helpful when negotiating a settlement.

CHAIN OF ASSETS

We were acting for a partially informed litigant. Early enquiries led us to a chain of assets spanning three continents and more than twenty live asset holdings or trading companies, as well as numerous trusts including holdings in land, factories, warehouses and plant, as well as a number of properties.

In both cases, being informed either before or early in the case was instrumental in achieving the litigants' aims.

At an early stage, it may be useful to consider the end-game if the divorce is likely to be hotly contested, with non-compliance and possibly a foreign element. It is worth working out at the start the nature and enforce-ability of any judgment that you could obtain in the country where the assets are either sited or controlled. Also worth analysing at an early stage is the discovery regime available in foreign countries. Some countries allow pre-action discovery to assist you in working out where to bring your claim.

Unlawfully obtained information

A common mistake is crossing the line between legiti-mate and illegitimate evidence gathering. It is impor-tant to stay on the right side of the law for a number of reasons.

1. Using unlawfully obtained documents and information is illegal and exposes you to penalties.

2. Such behaviour compromises the integrity and independence of lawyers and can lead them to be pushed off the case, in which case a new team has to be briefed at considerable expense.

3. Courts now realise that spouses who are successful in business have rights like everybody else; they are not necessarily going to default or behave unlawfully, and if they do, the law offers ways to compel disclosure. For example, if good evidence exists that documents or assets are likely to be dissipated or destroyed, then restraining and search orders can be highly effective and may be a necessity.

4. Arguments over admissibility can totally eclipse the main issue and drive up costs: you can spend as much time arguing over admissibility as you would otherwise have spent dealing with the divorce and sometimes, given the array of legitimate tools, it can be more than counterproductive.

The rules in relation to documentation (and other evidence) that has been unlawfully obtained have changed considerably. After 1992, the 'Hildebrand Rules' (England and Commonwealth countries) were interpreted as permitting a divorcing spouse to access documents belonging to the other spouse, whether confidential or not, provided force was not used. Once access had been gained, (s)he could keep and use copies (not the originals), but those copies had to be disclosed. Since 2010, the 'Hildebrand Rules' cannot be relied upon to justify, or provide a defence for, conduct which would otherwise be criminal or actionable at law. For example, if a person reads, copies or uses a confidential document without the authority of the document holder, they may commit an actionable breach of confidence, especially if it is shown to a third party. A spouse whose confidential information has been purloined is entitled to the same relief as anybody else would be.

Non-disclosing spouses

As mentioned earlier non-disclosure is common. Apart from the usual litigation armoury, third-party discovery orders are a great help and they are very much part of the machinery in divorces. If the other side cannot find their pension plans, bank statements or other financial documents (perhaps the dog has eaten them), you can get a court order to view or obtain documents from a third party: bank, trustee, pension fund manager. This sort of approach saves a lot of time and money, and does not enable the other side to wriggle, hide or dissemble.

The other thing to remember is to stick to your guns and not go to trial until the picture is complete. Non-disclosure is the enemy of both justice and finality. Matrimonial cases get reopened at vast expense and trauma when one party has not disclosed all the first time around.

Over-ambitious and misguided spouses are also common. A biologist's husband may convince himself that, though his wife did surveys for the local wildlife trust for twenty years, she has hidden enormous wealth.

This sort of thing is a pain to deal with. One technique is early and complete disclosure. A lot of information can be contained in bank statements. The English judiciary have in some ways become much better at insisting on relevance and proportionality; it is not unusual to be asked 'Do you need this and what are the facts the application/allegation is going to be based on?' Unfortunately, you can still end up with appalling injustices.

Fishing expeditions, time wasting and poor-quality advisers means sometimes the advisers end up with most of the family money. I have seen this happen all too often.

Money is a crucial aspect of divorces. Most systems now ascribe little or no importance to conduct during the marriage; for example, adultery (often a source of great personal angst) is seen as a symptom and not a cause. If a marriage has broken down then courts try to get everybody on their way as quickly and cheaply as possible, but a man or woman scorned can be a vicious opponent, making up, imagining or reimagining grotesque and perverse behaviour. It is horrible, unnecessary and can do unfathomable harm. Such allegations have to be dealt with in the way you would a criminal case – some even give rise to criminal cases, the consequences of which may be completely un-thought-out. If, say, the sole income provider ends up in jail and the family had few or no savings, it is hard to see that anything beneficial has been achieved at all.

If a spouse is guilty of serious criminality then that is a matter for the criminal courts to sort out. If it has happened then the proper consequences should follow, of course: but the criminal courts are not equipped to take children or other dependants into account.

Emotional fallout

Having mentioned psychological drivers, one of the things my firm has always done is have a list of therapists available for both parties. Divorces hurt; even if you are getting rid of or being relieved of an unsatisfactory and unpleasant spouse it is still an emotional wrench and your advisers ought to factor that in. The more help and assistance both spouses receive from friends, family and professional psychological advisers the better, it takes the angst out of the process and enables everybody to do what needs to be done as non-contentiously as possible. The importance of looking after the human beings cannot be overstated, particularly where there has been a betrayal and a threat to financial stability. Vengeful or distressed litigants can lose the ability to make rational decisions. This may or may not be a short-term phenomenon but there are often four recognised stages:

1. Denial

2. Anger

3. Depression

4. Acceptance

Some disadvantaged spouses are in danger of reloading. At a deep level, they do not accept that they have been betrayed or that their marriage is over, and then they can be easily manipulated into highly disadvantageous behaviour and settlements, especially if they break away from their advisers.

Funding

Complex disputes over large quantities of money are expensive to deal with. Sometimes the spouses are on a level playing field and sometimes not; sometimes quite aggressive steps need to be taken early to prevent dissipation, manipulation, destruction of documents and removal of assets, while simultaneously creating a fighting fund.

In most countries, it is forbidden to use litigation funders (see Chapter 6) in matrimonial disputes, especially before judgment. Under certain circumstances they can be used to collect unpaid final judgments, especially where there is a foreign element.

Even specialist matrimonial firms limit the number of cases that they deal with. Few specialist firms are large enough to extend credit; most do not want to do so and even larger firms will not, owing to the risks of non-payment. I have only encountered one specialist firm that would extend credit; it nearly always acts for disadvantaged wives of rich husbands, and is based in America where CFAs are fairly common (see Chapter 6). Sometimes a quick win at an early stage can provide a fighting fund and some lenders will provide credit to disadvantaged spouses where security for the credit can be offered.

Some jurisdictions will allow maintenance to be increased in order to take into account the level of legal fees that are necessary in HNW divorces. However, diverting maintenance to help with fees is not always a perfect solution.

Courts, particularly courts that do not deal with HNW matrimonial disputes regularly, may put pressure on the parties to conclude their business and one of the ways that they can do that is to cut the budget. Sometimes the budget needs to be large enough to permit a number of activities which are simply beyond what the court in question is used to dealing with. This can lead to tension over determining maintenance and timetabling.

SOLE TRADER

The litigant was a sole trader, the residual value of his business being very low because anybody buying the business would need to replace the person who was doing the work, at a not insubstantial salary. Undeterred, the other side produced an accountant who valued the business on a multiple of gross income, not net, then continued to maintain this was what it was worth. It was not (nobody would have paid that much for it). I asked pointedly, 'Who would buy it?' The accountant stuck to his guns, the judge accepted the valuation and I managed to get the litigant out with his shirt on, but only just.

WHERE'S THE MONEY?

In a case for much more money, in relation to a rather more complex business which did have a residual value, the opposition alleged that proprietor had hidden some money and had more income than she disclosed. Our immediate question was where did the extra income come from and where did it go, bearing in mind that every piece of paper and bank statement that she ever had anything to do with had been disclosed by this stage? Out came an expert witness and the court was bamboozled. This was absolutely devastating from my client's point of view. She ended up being assessed on the basis of money she simply never had.

CONCLUSION

- Settlement on agreed terms gives control over the results.

- Stay firm but fair all the way through.

- Do not tolerate non-disclosure.

- Do not tolerate fishing expeditions.

- Human beings need to be treated humanely.

10

Derivative Claims: Suing Your Company's Directors/ Shareholders

Duties of care

Derivative actions and breach of trust claims (Chapter 11) come together since they have several concepts in common. Both shareholders and beneficiaries 'own' the mismanaged assets indirectly, and both have rights and are owed obligations by the person(s) who have legal ownership, title or control of the assets.

Also, both shareholders and beneficiaries have rights to call for information about the assets. All of these rights stem from the fact that one or more person(s) is, in some fashion, in control of assets which they do not own. Accordingly, the law compensates by providing rights to monitor and gain recompense.

The usual litigation principles and parameters apply; however, there are variations.

When a person or entity manages or control the assets of others, obligations are imposed by both statutory and common law and by the governing documents, which might be a trust deed or a company's Articles of Association. In every part of the civilised world there are a series of statutes and cases conferring rights to gain information and to hold directors, controllers and trustees to account.

Calling for information

In all situations the putative plaintiff is entitled to call for information about 'their' assets. This step can be taken before launching litigation, giving access to information and documentation before deciding whether or not to sue.

The right to demand and receive information is therefore key. In practice, when directors/controllers/trustees have misbehaved, been incompetent or stolen assets, they are likely to blither, bluster and delay but the first thing to do is look at the rights to call for information and documentation. Every jurisdiction of which I am aware that has trust law places duties on trustees to account to the beneficiaries, within a reasonable period, and also to answer questions.

If you end up in any sort of litigation, let alone difficult and lengthy litigation, the judge ought to pick up on the fact if information was not forthcoming when requested, whether because its controllers could not or would not supply it. That starts to put the plaintiff (you) on the front foot.

Trusts are opaque; they do not normally file publicly accessible accounts. However, beneficiaries are entitled to ask for accounts for the trust and for any underlying companies, and for a lot more than the bare accounts, and to ask what has happened to assets and generally. As one judge put it:

> 'The plaintiffs had a right to request and the trustee had a duty to supply the trust accounts and a full inventory of the general trust assets. "Accounts" would be given a wide construction and it would be ordered that the defendants should supply the plaintiffs with copies of any accounts, documents or correspondence relating to the administration and execution of the trust, in addition to a

full inventory of trust assets and information concerning dealings with any real property.'[32]

Turning to companies, it is axiomatic that under the Articles of Association and the laws of the land where the company is incorporated, shareholders are entitled to call for information, to see the accounts and to ask questions of the directors.

If you think that anything is awry the first thing to do is to become better informed. If you know something is wrong and you are getting the runaround, do not get hung up on it because you should win the support of the court if you say to it, well I think this happened but I do not know and they will not tell me. Courts see deliberate non-disclosure so often that in many cases they can be relied upon to be quite terse with non-disclosers.

Public companies in most countries have publicly available accounts; private companies rarely do; the position 'offshore',[33] unless you are a shareholder, can be prove difficult indeed because the whole economy

---

32 *West v Lazards Bros & Co Jersey Limited* [1993] JLR 165
33 In some low tax areas, different rules apply to 'onshore' (ie. locally established and run) and 'offshore' companies, which might be incorporated locally but are foreign-owned and controlled.

hinges on a measure of opacity. Never mind accounts, lists of shareholders may not be available at all (eg Guernsey) or be hidden behind nominees (eg Jersey). What follows in relation to companies assumes you own shares in the company, directly or indirectly.

Companies

Minority shareholders in companies are at a disadvantage when trying to obtain recourse for perceived injustices within the administration of their company. There are three situations in which they might obtain a remedy:

1. A *personal action* between the wronged shareholder and another shareholder, or a director, or the company

2. A *derivative action*, where the minority shareholder stands in the place of the company to take steps against a third party on behalf of all the shareholders

3. An *unfair prejudice action*, where the wronged shareholder challenges some conduct of the company which is unfairly prejudicial to some or more of its shareholders

Derivative actions

Companies, as a matter of law everywhere that I am aware of, have a legal existence separate from that of the shareholders and the directors. *Foss v Harbottle [1843] 67 ER 189* ruled that, where a company suffers a wrong, only a claim brought by the company can remedy that wrong; that is logical. However, where a shareholder considers that the company has been wronged by those in control of it, those are the people who have the right to pursue the remedy. Turkeys will not vote for Christmas in October, so the company will resist bringing a claim, as those who committed the wrong will not direct the company to launch a claim against themselves. Hence the need for a 'derivative' action.

Before you consider such an action see if it is possible to marshal enough votes to replace the present directors with new ones. If that fails look at a derivative action.

A derivative action permits a minority shareholder to act as a representative of all the shareholders (whether some like it or not) and bring proceedings on behalf of the company to seek a remedy for a wrong perpetrated by those in control of the company. Unfortunately, in practice it remains difficult for minority shareholders to secure a court's permission to bring a derivative action. Because companies would be unmanageable if any shareholder could bring a derivative action at any time, the courts have imposed a number of obstacles. The principal question a court will consider in deciding whether to grant leave to bring a derivative action is whether the alleged wrong would go unchallenged if the derivative action was not brought. Thus, an application for leave to bring such an action must show that:

1. A wrong has been done to the company while under the control of the wrongdoers

2. The wrongdoers benefited from the wrong

3. There is no way of remedying this state of affairs other than permitting the minority shareholder to bring the derivative action

4. The action is reasonable, prudent and in the interests of the company

5. There is a realistic prospect of it succeeding at a full trial

When you have access only to the documents a shareholder can obtain about a company, the first two parts of the test can be difficult to meet. At this stage a lot can hinge on front-end load – follow the money and write open letters of enquiry to those you think have harmed the company, start with open source intelligence then move on to human intelligence.

The next two parts also present a number of problems. The court will only grant leave to bring a derivative action on behalf of a company if it is satisfied that you have exhausted all other remedies available; in particular, that you have held, or tried to hold, a shareholders' extraordinary meeting before you sought the leave of the court. At such a meeting, you should highlight the complaint to the other shareholders so that they can vote on whether to set aside the transaction(s) complained about or authorise the company to bring the action. The application for leave will be deemed premature if no attempt has been made to hold an extraordinary meeting. Where you made attempts but could not muster sufficient support to convene an extraordinary meeting, the court may be minded to order an extraordinary meeting to be called, before authorising a derivative action.

Even if you overcome all of these obstacles, a court may still refuse to permit the derivative action to proceed. You must also show that the proposed action has a realistic prospect of success, and even if it does the court may withhold leave where it disapproves of your conduct, or you have delayed bringing the application, or you previously approved the conduct against which you are now complaining.

A significant disadvantage to the derivative action is that if any damages are awarded, they accrue to the company, and the minority shareholder's interest therein is not directly dependent upon the success of the action – the damages will go to the company. If the action fails, any costs are ordered against the shareholder who instigated the claim, so you might have only a small stake in the upside benefit and be landed with all of the downside risk. It is not uncommon for the litigation arithmetic to be very finely balanced. The company could, of course, agree to indemnify you for your costs but that may be hard to achieve in practice.

Unfair prejudice actions

The rule in *Foss v Harbottle* prohibits minority shareholders from interfering in the management of the company, even where it is poorly managed and even when that causes them detriment: the majority rules, and ordinarily this state of affairs can and should only be rectified by shareholders voting to do so, ie a majority.

At this stage some common-sense advice is blindingly obvious – do not get into bed with people that you do not know or trust.

Unfair prejudice actions are an exception to the rule in *Foss v Harbottle*. They exist to provide a remedy for minority shareholders whose interests in the company have been, or will be, unfairly prejudiced by some action the company has taken or intends to take, for example where that action has been occasioned or sanctioned by majority shareholders whose interests diverge from the minority shareholders. A common situation giving rise to difficulty are contracts between the company and directors who also hold the majority voting rights.

There is no statutory definition of 'unfair prejudice'. However, an unfair prejudice action has, self-evidently, two elements: unfairness and prejudice. A company's acts may be unfair without prejudicing a minority shareholder, or may prejudice a minority shareholder without being unfair. In such cases, the unfair prejudice action will not offer a remedy. An unfair prejudice action may be brought in relation to acts already done or acts intended, but not yet carried out.

The tests, both of unfairness and of prejudice, are objective, not subjective. A starting point is always to examine the Articles of Association. Even if these have been complied with by the majority, the company's conduct could be unfairly prejudicial if any powers were not exercised for the benefit of the company as a whole, or you can show a breach of something you legitimately expect that is not formally described in the company's governing documents.

Proving 'legitimate expectation' is difficult. Companies exist under their Articles and other constitutional documents and internal rules (such as shareholder agreements). It may not be easy to show that it is legitimate to expect something where the facts behind your claim do not amount to breaches of the documented rules, and operating documents of the company. A legitimate expectation has been found where a shareholder was deprived of the ability to take part in decision-making despite a belief that they would be so allowed. By contrast, in a case where a shareholder sold their shares without the consent of the other shareholders, this was deemed not to relate to the company's affairs so, even though the company's documents gave the other shareholders a legitimate expectation to be asked to consent to such a sale (this is fairly unusual, except in small or family companies), that expectation was held to be unprotected by the test for unfair prejudice.

It is not necessary to show that those who caused the unfair prejudice were motivated by, or acted in, bad faith. An action does not have to be unlawful to be unfair. Equally, unlawfulness does not always amount to unfairness.

However, it is generally true that successful unfair prejudice applications are based either on a breach of the company's Articles of Association and related provisions, or where those terms are used in a manner which equity would regard as contrary to good faith. Context is important. What is fair between two competing businessmen might not be fair between members of a family. The alleged conduct must affect your interest as a shareholder; any other interest you may have in the company is irrelevant (so if you have bought its products, and it changes the after-sales servicing, that might affect your interest as a customer but not your interest as a shareholder).

Examples of unfair prejudice

The following are the types of matter which can amount to unfair prejudice:

- Exclusion from management, especially in a small, quasi-partnership context

- Declaring inadequate dividends

- Directors' excessive pay

- Failure to file or provide information

- Improper allocation of shares

- Discriminatory rights issues

- Diverting funds and business opportunities

- Mismanagement

- Unfair share valuation

- The conduct of the board, viewed as a whole

If unfair prejudice is found, the courts have a wide discretion as to what relief can be ordered. However, the remedy most often sought and granted is an order that one or more shareholders must buy the shares of one or more other shareholders. The game is only worth the candle if the price is right.

Although usually the majority is ordered to purchase the shares of the minority, that does not have to be the case. It has been held that a third party, who is not a shareholder, should be added to the action and then ordered to buy the shares of the minority. The court will take into account all the circumstances of the matter when deciding how to invoke this remedy; who founded the company, the roles of the parties in building it, any special qualifications required for running it and whether dishonesty or bad faith is found.

AN EXAMPLE

I acted for a hospitality industry professional, an old-school grafter, barely literate in his own language let alone English. He bought a 33% stake in a company which owned five good hotels and worked all the hours that God sent and more. His co-owners all had other businesses. My litigant was in hock to his eyeballs, every penny from the modest salary that he got from managing the hotels, which he part-owned, was used in the business and for his own maintenance.

The joint shareholders tried to sack him and take his shares for nothing. This was so obviously a species of fraud that we managed to obtain injunctions and in due course make the other shareholders pay one-third of the true value of the assets. This was a very lucky, very just, but unfortunately rare outcome.

Going forward, our litigant found a reputable partner, we found him a shareholders' agreement with all the appropriate checks and balances in, and he has never looked back. All has been good, but he could have been left with absolutely nothing. Had he started with a proper shareholders' agreement, he would have been in a much better position.

Valuing the shares to be bought or sold can become an issue. The court may order the valuer not to apply a discount to reflect the fact that the minority lacks control over the company (normally the degree of control would be reflected in the price). Valuations may be quite subjective and a wide range may be permissible.

Sometimes there is no appropriate relief. Where this has been found, the court may permit the applicant to amend their application to seek to wind up the company, another long and expensive process which might or might not produce money at the end.

CONCLUSION

If all of this seems to be depressingly complex, uncertain of outcome, difficult, time-consuming and expensive to progress, that is because it is.

A minority shareholding in a private company is generally worthless until converted into cash.

The points to take away from this summary are:

- Be highly cautious of investing time or money in small private companies.

- Do not get into bed with people you do not know, have not vetted, who have conflicting interests, have been sued before or have no relevant industry experience.

- Many of the ills inherent in this type of investment can be not so much cured but guarded against by bringing in a shareholders' agreement when you first invest.

- Lawyers are a cheap prophylactic but an expensive post-coital treatment. Shareholder agreements are common and try to make sure that the minority shareholders cannot be disadvantaged because they are a minority.

- A good starting place is value. To give a simple example, if there are 1,000 shares in a company worth £1 million, crude logic would say that each share is worth £1,000. How companies are valued is worthy of a treatise in itself. In practice, without a shareholders' agreement, each share is utterly worthless:

more shares can be sold, diluting the value of your holding; profits can be retained or diverted; the company can be liquidated and the assets sold too cheaply; or the company could be amalgamated with another company, at which stage your shares would be an even smaller percentage.

- Shares which do not carry minority protection or have attendant rights can be worthless: there is no market for them if nobody wants them.

- Preventative measures should include:

  - Non-dilution clauses, ie no more shares to be sold without unanimous shareholder approval

  - Tag-along rights so if the company amalgamates the smaller shareholders rights are preserved

  - Pre-emption rights to prevent issuing shares to other people without unanimous shareholder consent

  - Prohibitions on directors having competing interests and activities

  - In-built dispute resolution methods

– Mandatory mediation and arbitration
clauses instead of court processes

And so the list goes on. There is an awful lot that
can be done before you invest, much more than
can be done afterwards, and it is important to
pick a specialist adviser in that area.

11

Suing Your Trustee

Trustees have duties to beneficiaries,[34] some of them imposed by the trust deed and others imposed by the law, be it statutory or common law. Common law is a series of 'precedents', usually decisions made by courts.

What is a trust?

Trusts have been recognised by law for hundreds of years. Accordingly, all common law jurisdictions have

---

34 A trust deed will define the people, or classes of person, entitled to 'benefits' (usually payments) from the trust: they are known as 'beneficiaries'.

seen the evolution of rules and regulations that govern the flow of information, accountability and payment.

At this stage it is worth mentioning that, although trust law originated in England, both as a concept and in practice, many offshore centres have more advanced case law and statutes because trusts have been formed in such huge numbers offshore to avoid tax onshore.

Put simply, a person or body 'settles' money or assets for the 'benefit' of named (or a defined class of) 'beneficiaries', and appoints trustees to safeguard those assets. Sometimes they are paid for doing so, usually out of the trust. In return they must protect the assets, put well-judged investment policies in place in many cases, make sure benefits are paid to named or defined beneficiaries *and no one else*, and a flow of information about the assets must be given to the beneficiaries. The core relationship is normally contained in the 'trust deed', which sets out the powers and duties of the trustee – in practice offshore, trust documents are often much of a muchness and they are nearly all 'discretionary', ie the trustee has as to who (of the beneficiaries, or class of beneficiaries) gets what, if anything.

Why are offshore trusts set up as discretionary? What does it mean? Decades ago the idea was hatched that, instead of saying that a trust was, for example, for Mr A and then his children, or for a class of people such as the members of a pension scheme and their families, the declared beneficiary would be a charity, with the trustee having discretion to add other beneficiaries and then give or not give them money. The idea was that beneficiaries could not be taxed on money they had no formal entitlement to, and likewise those funds could not be attacked by creditors. To operate, these arrangements, of which there are many, need at least a nod and a wink between trustee, 'settlor' and beneficiaries.[35] There is a tension between the formal tax position, that the assets are owned by an offshore corporation, and the expectations of the person or family which originally settled the trust.

Not unnaturally HMRC and other tax bodies eventually came to take a dim view of this and reacted accordingly.

There are a multitude of variations. The duties of trustees in Jersey are as follows:[36]

---

35 In case this is not obvious, the settlor is the person or body that established the trust and provided the funds or other assets.
36 Article 21 of the Trusts (Jersey) Law (1984) as amended

1. A trustee shall in the execution of his or her duties and in the exercise of his or her powers and discretions:

   (a) act –

      i. with due diligence,

      ii. as would a prudent person,

      iii. to the best of the trustee's ability and skill; and

      iv. observe the utmost good faith.

2. Subject to this Law, a trustee shall carry out and administer the trust in accordance with its terms.

3. Subject to the terms of the trust, a trustee shall –

   (a) so far as is reasonable preserve the value of the trust property;

   (b) so far as is reasonable enhance the value of the trust property.

4. Except –

   (a) with the approval of the court; or

   (b) as permitted by this Law or expressly provided by the terms of the trust, a trustee shall not –

i. directly or indirectly profit from the trustee's trusteeship;

ii. cause or permit any other person to profit directly or indirectly from such trusteeship; or

iii. on the trustee's own account enter into any transaction with the trustees or relating to the trust property which may result in such profit.

5. A trustee shall keep accurate accounts and records of the trustee's trusteeship.

6. A trustee shall keep trust property separate from his or her personal property and separately identifiable from any other property of which he or she is trustee.

Jersey, for all its vicissitudes, has a very good trust law which balances things out well between beneficiaries and trustees. It has become the offshore equivalent of the gold standard. Duties imposed by law are ordinarily capable of abrogation, ie being varied in governing documents, but Jersey's statute pre-empts that: any very clauses inserted in the trust deed (or in deeds by which trustees resign or are appointed) seeking to impose overly extensive limits on the trustee's obligations are invalid. Therefore, clauses saying 'you cannot sue us (the trustees) whatever we do' are not effective and there are limits on how far a trustee who steps down or distributes funds to a beneficiary can claim to have discharged their duty.

The rest of this chapter applies where there is a level playing field: a proper balance between the trustees' duties to the beneficiaries, their being able to get on and do their job without constantly having to look over their shoulder, and the 'standard rights' that the deed usually confers on potential plaintiff beneficiaries. There are some rabbit holes – beneficiaries might not be clearly named (or defined) in the deed; they might only appear in a side letter or similar – but there are normally ways around that if you are thinking about suing trustees.

The information that trustees must make available has often been litigated, in many places. Fundamentally, beneficiaries are entitled to a lot more than a simple set of accounts, particularly as in the great scheme of things accounts always come after the event (that is their nature) and are usually brief.

This is well-worn territory. There is a lot you can require a trustee to disclose to you. If a simple request does not do it then courts, particularly courts that have dealt with these issues before, tend to be wearied of trustees who withhold information. If information has been withheld then courts tend to extend the periods within which you could bring an action. You could apply to fire the trustee and replace them/it with a more competent or impartial entity.[37] This has two advantages: the new trustee gets to see a lot of information as it is handed over and may show it to you; and the incoming trustee has a fresh period within which to bring proceedings against its predecessor.

If you suspect a breach of the terms of the trust applications for information should be couched as stand-alone applications: this is an application for trust accounts, you are not claiming a breach of trust (yet). In practice, beneficiaries often know more or less what has happened or have an inkling. Sometimes you may have to get on and start action to meet time limits. Breaches of trust are failures by trustees; they might be simple mistakes, they might be badly motivated.

Jersey and the other Channel Islands are home to many trusts: it is a big industry which has given rise to a lot

37 Trustees might be individuals but are often companies: many banks run trustee companies, the better ones are ordinarily independent.

of litigation. My firm has recovered tens of millions of pounds for disappointed beneficiaries over the last three decades.

RIGHTS TO INFORMATION

Thirty years ago, the trust industry's attitude was often secretive. We knocked the door down many years ago in a case called *West v. Lazards Brothers & Co (Jersey) Ltd [1993] JCR.*

Mr West was an entrepreneur. At his suggestion, a company within a trust he had set up bought a piece of land which was primed to come up for planning permission, using loans. Mr West and the trust ran out of money. A deal was brokered under which a man called Pike would pay off the mortgage and the trust would retain a share in the land.

A bank owned the trustee, and Mr Pike was a friend of the manager. Instead of paying off the mortgage it was transferred to a new vehicle, leaving Mr West's trust effectively with nothing. To add insult to injury the bank then tried to evict Mr West from another property which he owned personally and in which he and his family lived, by calling in the guarantee on a loan that Mr Pike had also agreed to pay off.

This was obvious skulduggery, but it took a long time to sort out – no fewer than eight solid months in court. The trustee was found to have behaved fraudulently. The case established several helpful principles in relation to beneficiaries' rights to information and set limits on trustees' scope to absolve themselves of liability. Since this case offshore trustees have been looking over their shoulders, which is no bad thing for beneficiaries.

Breaches of trust are usually more mundane: failing to insure the trust property, giving assets to the wrong people, losing investments, making bad investments, investing in the trustees' own companies. What you might suspect to be nepotism might be no more than ineptitude. Since the law expects trustees to be competent and careful no one other than a fully insured professional should take a trusteeship on; well-meaning assistance to family members can lead to vicious and expensive litigation with personal liabilities being imposed on folk who intended harm to nobody.

In many jurisdictions where trusts are big business the trustee has to carry insurance and be a corporate body with at least two suitably qualified directors.

Trusts and what can go wrong

Offshore trusts are often sold as 'wrappers' for someone's affairs, to protect their assets, to help manage tax and to preserve assets for future generations.

Where it commonly goes wrong is where the settlor is treated as a client,[38] and the trustee does as the settlor tells it. If the settlor makes a mess of their own affairs held in the trust structure, the trustee faces being sued by the settlor (because it should have exercised independence) and the beneficiaries (who are often family members).

Other fertile sources of litigation tend to be where in-house products are sold to the trust by a trustee's associated companies – I cover this in the next part of this chapter.

What about a trust deed that does not clearly define beneficiaries, for example a trust with 'discretion' to pay the Red Cross or another charity, which will never know of the trust's existence (because, often, it was never intended to)? How does the court sort it out? Well,

---

38 NB The settlor may also be a beneficiary under some trusts.

the beneficiary is normally pretty obviously the litigant; it might be possible to establish who the beneficiaries were *supposed* to be. From an offshore perspective, *Schmidt v. Rosewood Trust Limited [2003] UKPC 261* (before the supreme court for the Commonwealth) does not make happy reading, but lower courts have taken it on board and are now pretty robust at disciplining trustees and recovering funds. This is what the Privy Council had to say:

> 'It has become common for wealthy individuals in many parts of the word (including countries which have no indigenous law of trust) to place funds at their disposition into trusts (often with a network of underlying companies) regulated by the law of, and managed by trustees resident in, territories with which the settlor (who may also be a beneficiary) has no substantial connection. These territories (sometimes called tax havens) are chosen not for their geographical convenience (indeed face to face meetings between the settlor and his trustees are often inconvenient) but because they are supposed to offer special advantages in terms of confidentiality and protection from fiscal demands (and sometimes from problems

under the insolvency laws, or laws restricting freedom of testamentary disposition, in the country of the settlor's domicile). The trusts and powers contained in a settlement established in such circumstances may give no reliable indication of who will in the event benefit from the settlement. Typically, it will contain very wide discretions exercisable by the trustees (sometimes only with the consent of a so-called protector) in favour of a widely-defined class of beneficiaries. The exercise of those discretions may depend on the settlor's wishes as confidentially imparted to the trustees and the protector. As a further cloak against transparency, the identity of the trust settlor or settlors may be concealed behind some corporate figurehead.'[39]

Their Lordships did not seem to be impressed.

Before dealing with what beneficiaries can do about a trust once it has gone wrong, it is worth looking in a little more detail at three scenarios where trusts go wrong with monotonous regularity:

---

39   *Schmidt v. Rosewood Trust Ltd* (2003), UKPC 261

1. In-house products

2. Portfolio losses

3. Partiality

In-house products

When the trustee is owned by a bank or investment house, its motivation at the outset may not be to provide trustee services for deserving beneficiaries but to acquire a wider client base for the sale of its own products, normally banking plus investment advice. No need to market; shoot the fish in the barrel.

People in this industry have told me that their privately owned trust company automatically conducts 'beauty parades' – compares its services to the trust structure, fees, investment policies and performance with those of competitor companies. This is obviously good trusteeship. However, from the day after the trust company was acquired by a bank or similar corporate, no one was allowed to meet a client without taking a private banker with them, to allow the private banker to sell the parent company's services.[40] Beauty parades became a thing of the past.

---

40 Who 'the client' is in these situations can be unclear.

If the trust loses money in this sort of scenario the trustee is put in an extremely difficult position, as it has an obvious and inherent conflict of interest.

Portfolio losses

These happen rather too often inside trust structures, either as a result of the trustee using its own products whether they are suitable for the trust or not, or where too much freedom of action has been delegated to investment managers, or where the activities of the investment manager have not been adequately scrutinised, particularly investment managers that are not independent of the trustee or its parent.

A trustee managing investments for which it is not qualified is obviously at risk of being sued as soon as any loss occurs. Few trustees are daft enough to do that these days, not least because their insurers discourage such behaviour. Investment management can and still does go horribly wrong, even with outside professional investment advisers: these may not be independent enough (eg from a bank) and/or monitoring may be inadequate.

Partiality

Under the trust deed trustees are supposed to remain impartial and neutral towards all the beneficiaries. In practice it is human to know and like one side better than another and difficult not to take decisions accordingly, leading to actions by the aggrieved parties.

Solutions

As well as the normal litigation basics, covered in some detail already, there are various steps you should take when dealing with trustees.

1. Litigant beneficiaries can and should *exercise your rights* to full accounts, promptly provided. In this day and age disclosure should be automatic but often it is not (my firm recently sued a trustee, owned by a bank, which could not produce accounts; a replacement had to be appointed, to produce these.)

2. *Ask for documentation.* Fundamentally, trust documents belong to beneficiaries and you are entitled to sufficient knowledge to hold the trustees to account.

3. *Query the accounts.* There is no need to accept the accounts as drawn, they can be queried and supporting documentation sought – accounts rely on accounting conventions so may over-simplify, eg assets might be valued at what was paid to buy them, not their present-day value. Sometimes a lot more information is needed.

4. Preferably in writing, *ask for explanations and/or actions.* If the trustee delays, obfuscates or fobs you off, then in some ways this might actively assist in the long term.

5. *Sack the trustee.* If you have good reason to doubt the *bona fides*, competence or capability of the trustee, or just do not get on with them (the relationship breaks down), you may demand they be replaced and the courts set a relatively low threshold for replacement.

6. *Choose any replacement trustee with care.* A competent replacement trustee can be a well-heeled and well-informed ally. A good incoming trustee will take extremely seriously its duties to:

   – Examine carefully what its predecessor has done;

   – Interrogate its predecessor as appropriate;

- Inform the beneficiaries of its findings; and

- In appropriate circumstances, take action against its predecessors to restore the trust fund.

7. You should now be in a position to *take fully informed and documented advice on available rights of action* having made use of your rights to information about what are, in effect, in whole or in part, 'your' assets.

CONCLUSION

Before embarking on suing a trustee, strengthen your hand by doing your homework. It is crucial to obtain full accounts and any related documentation. Properly scrutinize the accounts, raise queries, ask the trustee to provide explanations and, if needed, supporting documentation. Remember, where grave doubts exist about the competence or suitability of the trustee, they can be removed from post. Ensuring that any replacement trustee is careful, competent, and rigorous will put you in the best possible position to take further action.

12

Making The Buggers Pay – Insurers

The title for this chapter came from a joint lecture that an English barrister (later a judge) gave some years ago. I sometimes suspect that I am unduly cynical, but according to a colleague from London, I remain somewhat naive.

In my experience, on the majority of occasions the insurance industry works well (and it would not function if it did not), and it does what it says on the packet. My colleague had a less rosy view: there is obviously a dark side to the insurance industry. A badly motivated and badly advised insurer is a formidable and shameless opponent.

This chapter sets out the inherent conflicts in that industry and gives some pointers to how to avoid getting into difficulty and then what to do about it if you do; by which I mean your insurance cover is revoked, your insurance does not cover you, or the insurer just will not pay. This last may be accompanied by a great deal of dissembling, threats and plain untruths. I give examples below.

Most of the claims I have dealt with have been in the commercial arena but two domestic incidents are also worthy of examination.

Conflicting interests

First of all, insurers are in effect bookmakers. They give the client a piece of paper which says 'I will pay you if…' Insurers realise that no one would buy insurance if they do not pay most of the claims that are submitted; but not all their staff realise this. The more policies they sell, the more money comes in; the fewer and smaller the claims they pay out the more money they keep. This is a fundamental conflict of interest; and managers chasing bonuses have been known to cut the price of the product and then sit on claims. This only works while they can get publicity for the first but manage to keep the second secret.

I have five pieces of advice for litigants at a very early stage:

1. If you use a broker, they are obliged to send you a *statement of demands and needs* before you pay any premium. Read it, check it, if there is anything you do not understand ask for clarification; and keep it if you decide to go ahead.

2. *Read the policy* when you get it, and work out what it says. They are often obscurely worded so that even professionals struggle to work out what they mean. If you do not understand what it says, write to your broker and ask for clarification, especially if it seems to differ from the statement of demands and needs. Do this long before you ever need to claim; ideally, do it when you get the policy documents.

3. *Are you insured?* This is one of the first questions I ask. Directors and managers forget that the company may have 'Directors & Officers' (D&O) cover and householders forget their household insurance may include legal expenses cover.

4. If you get anywhere near an insured claim, *immediately warn the broker (or insurer,* if you do not use a broker) and establish a working

relationship. Underwriters and their advisers can be very helpful. Conversely, if you take action which they have not authorised in advance, then insurers may not pay for it.

5. Remember: *the broker works for you*. Their job is to make sure you get the best cover for the best price and to help make sure that claims are handled properly. In practice, they can work hand in glove with insurance companies who are, in effect, their paymasters. It can be difficult to work out who actually pays the broker and where they make their money. Commissions are structured to encourage long-term relationships, which might not work in your interest. Other problems can arise from the nature of the industry and human nature.

Problems with domestic policies

As I said earlier, most of my work has been in the commercial arena but let us look at some domestic policies.

My wife went out and insured our vehicles, back came a cover note. I asked for the policy. I read it with amazement. The policy said that you (the insured) are not insured for commuting (ie going to work) or even driving to a place of study. My wife did not know this limit was in place. If you don't know, ask. If you use a broker, this ought to be prominent on the statement of demands and needs.

Equally worrying was the clause that said, 'You must tell us *immediately* if you have an accident'. People who have been involved in serious accidents sometimes spend several days in hospital before they regain their wits; phoning their insurers is not top of their list. This clause was being used to great effect in order not to pay out, so the client had bought a policy, been run into and then denied cover as they were too sick or confused to immediately call the broker.

Personally, when I get an insurance policy, I read it. Most people do not. If the broker you are using does not tell you clearly what they are selling you, then get another broker.

Some years ago, in relation to my own motor policy, my broker wrote to me and said, I would be pleased to know they had included a 'keys clause'. Intrigued, I asked for a copy of the policy and looked at the 'keys clause' that was softly being advanced as some form of advantage to me. It said, if you leave the keys in the car or you lose them you are not insured. I said thank you but no thank you; I would only have to make a momentary mistake in the wrong environment and lose both my car and my insurance. The broker should have warned me not to touch this policy.

REMIND YOUR BROKER WHO THEY WORK FOR

Some years ago, I was consulted by a respectable, long-established firm who had, fortuitously, bought motor insurance from their regular broker for a maintenance employee.

One of the properties that they maintained burned down. Accident investigators sent by the insurer blamed the maintenance man (who denied their assertion): in other words, they said the fire was my client's fault. At this point, the broker wrote that it had 'agreed' with underwriters that my client was not insured, as their policy on the property could be interpreted as not covering the activities of the maintenance man.

I pointed out that, since the broker undoubtedly knew that my client was doing maintenance works – after all, they had insured the car and met the maintenance man – the broker needed to pay, because they had been negligent in not arranging the right cover to match their client's business.

After a brief silence, we received a fresh letter from the broker saying it had re-examined matters with underwriters, who were pleased to write out a cheque in full.

A good result for my client but an example of shameless collusion and complete dereliction of duty by the broker.

Engaging with underwriters and making sure you are covered

I said earlier if you are anywhere near claiming on insurance you really do need to give underwriters a heads-up at the start and if possible, build a relationship. Sometimes they can be very helpful indeed.

The first point to realise is that, if you are running a business complaints can arise. Whether those complaints have any merit or not, underwriters need to be told and updated on a regular basis. First of all you are being transparent with them, which you almost certainly agreed to do on the proposal form. This means they know which types of risks they are underwriting: if you show that you handle complaints well, so that claims rarely arise, they might see you as a better risk than they initially thought, and premiums might come down. Secondly, it means that if a complaint later develops into a claim they cannot say you are not insured because you did not tell us as soon as the claim was possible. Moreover, by always telling them you now have documented records of handling complaints so that they do not lead to claims, which could be useful if you eventually do have to claim. Despite all this, some underwriters may wriggle.

Here are two examples of how this works in practice.

OFF THE RAILS

My firm sued another lawyer who was in the middle of a divorce and had few, if any, visible assets, so we were banking on him being insured – it is mandatory for some professions to be insured.

Sadly, this is a prime example of how to vitiate your cover. The lawyer first ignored all letters. After a delay we started to receive pre-action responses from a large firm of Advocates (who the lawyer could not have afforded), then they stopped writing to us, saying they no longer acted. We learned the lawyer had not kept his insurers up to date, and they had declined cover.

A NONSENSICAL CLAIM

A professional firm was faced with a nonsensical claim – by this I mean a bad claim which was not justified. Early correspondence went off to underwriters, who appointed competent London solicitors to deal with the matter and advise. In conjunction with the solicitors, the underwriters took the view that there were no merits in the claim, but that this was a determined litigant, so they paid some blood money to get rid of it. This was of considerable benefit to the insured, and the whole matter was dealt with pragmatically, honestly and competently, not only by the underwriters but also by their advisers.

Now having looked at how it goes right, let us have another look at how it can go wrong.

MORE WRIGGLING

Fraud on insurers is a massive problem, so they have whole departments dealing with fraudulent claims. When they think they are being scammed, insurers dig their heels in, and who can blame them. Unfortunately, they sometimes think they are being scammed when they are not.

A hedge fund manager had two houses, one of which was empty, so he advised insurers that he was not living there, that it was boarded up and that he was thinking of rebuilding if he got planning permission. Along came an arsonist and set fire to his house. Did the insurers pay? No, not until sued.

The insurers brought in specialist solicitors who tried to blame our litigant for the fire; when that failed, they alleged dishonesty on the basis that the litigant had no coherent plan for redevelopment, based on some extraordinary claims by a series of surveyors who were not involved in the proposed development.

My firm got the litigant some compensation in the end but it was an unhappy experience, mainly because, in my view, the insurers had put it into the fraudulent claim category because it was an arson attack. As a result, they were unwilling to countenance payment, even though everyone accepted that the insured was not the arsonist.

REGULATORS

We were consulted by the directors of a leveraged income fund. A leveraged income fund is by definition high-risk. Fund units were sold to sophisticated investors with the appropriate health warning. There was an unexpected movement of

the market and half of the fund became worthless.
These things happen.

In this case the regulator hired a specialist QC
from London who made a number of unsustainable
allegations and criticisms. The fund's directors
had D&O cover, so I sent a disclosure letter to the
underwriters, who refused to pay, giving no reasons.
At this stage we diverted our attention to fending off
the regulator which we did in relatively short order.

Throughout that process we kept the insurers
informed, even though they had told us they were
not going to pay; they received copies of all bills,
client care letters, and we told them what we were
doing, in what order and why. I had in mind a clause
in the policy (this is fairly common) to the effect that
'if we do not authorise something then we will not
pay for it'. As they were not authorising anything, we
were obviously going to have a tussle at some stage,
but we kept them informed.

When we got to the end, we submitted a bill; the
underwriters replied that they had not authorised
our work so would not pay. Our client proceeded to
sue them. The underwriters then claimed that, at the
time the policy was renewed, the fund had been in
breach of its banking covenants and not informed
the underwriter; but my client was able to produce
letters to the underwriters saying, 'We are in breach
of the banking covenants at the moment, does this

vitiate our D&O cover?', to which the underwriters had replied, 'Please send the premium, you are covered'.

In short, the underwriters were trying to wriggle out of cover they had agreed to provide. After a writ in the High Court in London the fund directors received a cheque by return.

Household insurance policies

The legal expense cover sold as an add-on to many household insurance policies does not always work well. I have seen it work and I have seen it fail. The underwriters may insist that you use lawyers that they tell you to use, but often the policy does not entitle them to do that – they will, however, try it on. This has resulted in Jersey-based policemen being given advice by English solicitors whose claim to fame was expertise in tractor leasing, or matrimonial law (in another case). Neither tractor leasing nor divorce was at issue. In these cases, the officers ended up paying out of their own pockets; but the action eventually succeeded.

In another case, a big claim, we advised that a proper claim assessment would cost about £3,000; the household insurers introduced a lawyer who offered to do it for £300. It ought to be obvious that £300 does not buy much time or expertise.

CONCLUSIONS

- When buying cover make sure you describe clearly, preferably in writing, the nature and extent of your business.

- At the outset, tell the underwriter of any allegations of wrongdoing, even where completely unfounded.

- Read the statement of needs and demands, also read the policy, not just the cover note; keep all of these; if in doubt raise specific written queries and get written answers.

- As soon as you are notified of what might lead to an insured claim, advise underwriters.

- If in doubt, remind any brokers you use whose side they are on.

- At the first hint of hesitancy or dissembling seek legal advice. Law can be a cheap and effective prophylactic, it is a lot more expensive once an action starts.

Acknowledgements

I am indebted to Advocate Robin Leeuwenburg and Advocate Steven Chiddicks for their assistance with the material for this book.

The Author

 Philip Sinel graduated from Middle Temple over thirty years ago and has been in both law and intelligence ever since, helping people and companies gain restitution, enforce their legitimate rights and avoid being taken to the cleaners.

The author is the founder and owner of Sinels Advocates, the founder of Sintel Global and founder of Sinels Global Restitution.

Sintel Global Limited provide intelligence services for both private and corporate litigants. Sinels Global Restitution has been extracting monies from recalcitrant debtors for over a decade.

- https://www.linkedin.com/in/philip-sinel -50048648/
- www.restitutionlimited.com
- www.sinels.com/
- https://sintelglobal.co.uk